///////NASCAR

Winston Cup

1993

FOREWORD

BILL FRANCE, JR.

....

T he NASCAR Winston Cup Series continued to grow in 1993. Great competition in every event, a tight championship points race and an intense chase for the Manufacturer's Championship highlight the 1993 NASCAR Winston Cup series season.

I don't have to tell anyone that 1993 was a tough year. We faced the tough times together, and we moved ahead.

The NASCAR Winston Cup Series competed for the first time at the New Hampshire International Speedway in Loudon, NH. Many of our teams also tested at Indianapolis Motor Speedway to prepare for the historic, inaugural Brickyard 400 there in 1994. At the New Hampshire race and

"WE ARE PROUD OF OUR FANS, BECAUSE THEY ARE THE MOST LOYAL IN MAJOR LEAGUE SPORTS."

the Indianapolis test, our new friends and fans made us feel welcome, and we're glad to be there.

The 1993 NASCAR Winston Cup Series season opened with five different winners in the first five races before Rusty Wallace, Dale Earnhardt, and Mark Martin each enjoyed win streaks. The race for the NASCAR Winston Cup Championship wasn't decided until the last race of the season again this year.

Fan enthusiasm and support for NASCAR and our marketing partners continues to grow. We are proud of our fans, because they are the most loyal in major league sports. We are grateful to our track operators and to our NASCAR Winston Cup drivers, owners, teams, and their sponsors for sharing our common commitment to excellence.

We are proud of the heritage of NASCAR racing. The pages that follow chronicle the intensity and determination of the 1993 NASCAR Winston Cup Series season.

ACKNOWLEDGMENTS

The 1993 NASCAR Winston Cup season was filled with peaks and valleys. We lost two of the premier drivers in Alan Kulwicki and Davey Allison and our sympathies go out to their families and loved ones. We also witnessed one of the most hard fought points races in recent history with Dale Earnhardt and Rusty Wallace going to the wire before deciding who would be named 1993 NASCAR Winston Cup Champion. Congratulations to Mr. Dale Earnhardt.

As always the people at NASCAR deserve an extra special thanks. All of them work tirelessly to bring you the most exciting racing in the country. Without their help and guidance this book would not be possible. Special thanks to Mr. Bill France Jr., Mr. Jim France, Mr. Brian France, Mr. Les Richter, Mr. Bill Seaborn, and Mr. Paul Schaefer.

All the members of the NASCAR Winston Cup team at the R. J. Reynolds Tobacco Co. deserve everyone's appreciation too. Thanks to Mr. Jim Johnston, Mr. T. Wayne Robertson, Mr. Jeff Byrd, Mr. John Powell, Mr. Steve Tucker, Mr. Ty Norris, Mr. Dennis Dawson, Mr. Randy Chapel, Mr. Jim Bowling, Mr. Lindsay Synder and Mr. Nat Walker.

Again this year Mr. Bob Kelly accepted the task of writing the NASCAR Yearbook. His knowledge is unsurpassed in the field of Motorsports and we are grateful for his efforts.

The photos in the NASCAR Yearbook are the work of several people, including Mr. Dozier Mobley, Mr. Ernie Masche, Mr. Mike Meadows, Mr. Kenny Kane, Mr. Brian Czobat, Mr. Jim Conover, Mr. Russ Hamilton, Mrs. Joanne Hamilton, Mr. Jerry Howell, and Mrs. Lynn Schneider. They worked hard to bring you just the right photos from every stop.

Finally and MOST IMPORTANTLY, thank you the NASCAR FAN. You are the reason this sport is the most exciting in the world.

PHOTO CREDITS:

•Jim Conover	•Brian Czobat	•Russ Hamilton	•Joanne Hamilton	•Jerry Howell
•Kenny Kane	•Ernie Masche	•Mike Meadows	•Dozier Mobley	•Lynn Schneider

---

Winston Cup '93 Staff: Ivan Mothershead, Publisher; Charlie Keiger, Associate Publisher; Merry Schoonmaker, Associate Publisher; Bob Kelly, Senior Editor; Amy Vail, Coordinator-Editor; Jason Simon and Jeff Huneycutt, Asst. Editors; Dozier Mobley, Bob Castanzo, Kenny Kane, Photo Editors; Brett Shippy and Mike McBride, Layout-Design

TABLE OF CONTENTS
'93

Davey Allison

> *"The group of real racers in the world is pretty small. Those of us who watched Davey come up through the ranks also remember when Kyle Petty was playing high school football, Sterling Marlin was changing his dad's tires, Mark Martin had Dennis the Menace painted on the side of his truck and Rusty Wallace was a wild-haired kid from around St. Louis. It's a tight-knit group with a lot of memories — and it's painful when someone has to leave early." — STEVE HMIEL*

Just a few days before he left us, Davey Allison said that for the first time in his life, everything was in order and in balance. His team was ultra-competitive on a week-to-week basis, his family life had taken on new luster after the move to a recently completed house, and his Catholic faith had come to life for him.

He took great pleasure from his family, particularly wife Liz and his children, Krysta, 3, and Robbie, 2. "We're having so much fun," he said at Daytona during a Pepsi 400 practice break. "I really didn't know it could be like this. It's wonderful."

A few short days later, NASCAR Winston Cup racing received a body blow with the news of Davey's death. The tightly-knit racing community had barely begun to heal the wounds left by the loss of Alan Kulwicki.

With Davey, it lost a link to the past — and one of the most highly-competitive people inside the garage area fence. He had the inner fire to win — and if it wasn't his day, he would fight just as hard for a position as he would for a victory. Strong-willed, he also had been brought up to be respectful.

And all who knew him will remember the mischievous streak that ran through him; the way his eyes would twinkle when he had a prank in mind.

In 1989, Davey participated in the benefit golf tournament preceding the second running of the Phoenix race. Playing with Robert Yates, David Ifft, team-member Lee McCall and NASCAR inspector Larry Childress, we rattled our way around The Wigwam course.

Davey wasn't much of a golfer then; he came to play for fun and to help the charities involved with the tournament. We came to a 150-yard par-three over water, with a Corvette waiting on the other side as a hole-in-one prize.

"I'm gonna win that car and then drive it to Dearborn and go see Michael Kranefuss (Ford's racing boss)," Davey said with a grin. We all grinned too, because we'd watched him try (for the most part, unsuccessfully) to hit a golf ball for more than two hours!

He gripped his five-iron baseball bat-style and proceeded to knock his ball within three inches of the cup. He fumed because it didn't go in the hole.

We made putts all day, and ended up winning the tournament with a 14-under score. That made absolutely no difference to Davey.

He was still fussing.

"I wanted to see the look on Kranefuss' face," he grinned with that impish look in his eyes.

And Kranefuss would have loved the visit.

The German-born boss of Ford's world-wide racing programs, Kranefuss had a special place in his heart for Davey.

"I've known a lot of drivers in a lot of different situations — both bad ones and good ones — but Davey was special," Kranefuss said afterward. "I think of all the drivers in Winston Cup racing, he's probably the one I had the closest relationship with.

"He was an Allison — and he always said what he thought. One thing I hate is people who beat around the bush. If we've got a problem we should be talking about it and get it over with.

That was never a problem with Davey.

"I could not believe that such a young person would have such a strong personality. Davey had his own world and his own way of doing things. He could be extremely aggressive and, at times, nagging. But it was never negative or demeaning — it was always constructive."

That forceful personality with the mischievous grin is gone. But any fan who ever met him will always remember the moment. He was an Allison, and his father taught him early in his life that the fans are the ones who support racing and make it possible for people like him to make their living from the sport.

That lesson was one he always kept foremost in his mind, and he always found time for the fans.

That may be the finest tribute of all.

Davey Allison
1961-1993

REMEMBERING....
Alan Kulwicki

> *"You are never given a dream without also being given the power to make it true. You may have to work for it, however."*
> —RICHARD BACH

Just a year ago, Alan Kulwicki sat in a vacant hospitality suite adjacent to the Atlanta press box, flushed with victory after winning the 1992 NASCAR Winston Cup championship. The accolades were over, the trophy his, the interviews completed. With two long-time friends, he talked of the accomplishments of his team during the season and ticked off the points he wanted to make in the Champion's Foreword for the 1992 edition of this book.

In the brief moments of that discussion, he changed. During those few minutes, one could see the import of the title begin to hit home. He talked of his philosophy of life, of working hard to obtain goals, of picking himself off the canvas after his team had suffered knock-down blows in their quest for the title.

He paused and began talking about the impossibility of the goal he had achieved in winning the title. He looked back within himself to see Hales Corners, and spoke of going back there when he had last been in Wisconsin, watching the drivers on the dirt track and wondering to himself how any driver could ever make it to Winston Cup from such an inauspicious beginning.

It was then that he spoke of how proud he was to have been able to even compete in NASCAR Winston Cup racing. How he had been so naive to think he could make it in this sport with two cars, two engines and two crew members in 1986. How he had stubbornly held onto his hope of making his own team work. How difficult it had been to find the right people with the same work ethic he had.

How fortunate he had been when others had attempted the same thing but had not been successful with their ventures.

And at that moment, he began to speak of the great opportunity that now belonged to him. The chance to be a good champion, to be someone who, a year later, the NASCAR community would feel had represented its sport with dedication — and a champion who had been good to the fans.

"I know from my experience in the sport," Alan said quietly, "that the chance to win a championship might never come to us again — either to me as a driver, or to us as a team. I want to be as good a champion as I can be, in case the chance never happens again."

Little did any of us know Alan's time as the champion would be so limited.

Since April 1, much has been said about the intensity Alan brought to the race track. He approached the opportunity to be the reigning Winston Cup Champion with that same combination of pride and stubbornness.

Winston Cup Series

NASCAR

1992
WINSTON CUP CHAMPION
ALAN KULWICKI

He made himself available, even on short notice, when asked by the folks at R.J. Reynolds or NASCAR for personal appearances or activities. He was not averse to picking up the phone and calling either group to ask, "What's next?" or "What can I do to help?"

Ever since he made his NASCAR Winston Cup debut in late 1985, his goals were to make the field at races, then to finish races, then to finish in the top-20, the top-10 and finally, to be competitive enough to win races. The dream of a Championship was tightly-held, and even to Alan, it seemed an impossibility unless he drove for one of the front-running teams.

In each instance, he accomplished what he set out to do, and the title won last year at Atlanta was the crowning step of his career.

It serves as an inspiration to every young driver — and to every person. Alan proved again that if one works hard enough, what appears to be impossible indeed becomes possible.

With the interview complete in the Atlanta hospitality suite, Alan stood and began walking toward the door. He turned and his dark eyes gleamed.

"Put this in there, somewhere," he said. "If what I have been able to accomplish in this sport by winning the Championship makes somebody dream bigger, work harder, and accomplish something they think they can't, then I'll feel I made an impact as the Champion."

Consider it done, Champ.

Alan Kulwicki

1954-1993

THE NASCAR WINSTON CUP CHAMPION 1993....

 ## DALE EARNHARDT

*E*very time you win a NASCAR Winston Cup Championship, it becomes more special. And this year, after winning the title in a super battle with Rusty, and after overcoming all the things that happened throughout the season, this sixth Winston Cup means an enormous amount to me — and to my team.

It's so hard to win the title. Unless you have gone through a championship battle, it's hard to make anyone else understand what it really takes to emerge at the end of the season as the leader in the points.

There are so many unknowns when you set out at the beginning of the season. Just to win a race takes great preparation and execution. The competition is so tight that any one small things can keep you from victory lane — and reward another driver and team who have it all together that week.

Winning isn't the only hard part. To go through the length of a season that we do, and to finish well at every race — on all the different types of tracks — really tests the people who make up the team. To fight with another team that is a quality group, and to battle with a driver who is just as competitive as you, and just as determined behind the wheel, and then to win over someone as good as him and them — is something in which you take great pride .

Those are the marks of a championship team. You must have every part perfect if you're going to be the Champions. And this

year we did. Last year, we didn't.

Last year in December, the only time I went to the stage at the Waldorf-Astoria was to accept membership in the McDonald's All Star Team. I was honored to be included, particularly after the season we had just finished. By our team's standards, we had a poor year — we finished 12th in the points. To us, with the great pride this team has in itself, our season had almost been an embarrassment. We had worked all year, thinking each week that the next week would be the one in which we turned it around and got back into the chase for the championship.

But it never happened. And when banquet time came, we found out just how it feels not to be the team being honored. Because of that, and because of the way we had struggled throughout the

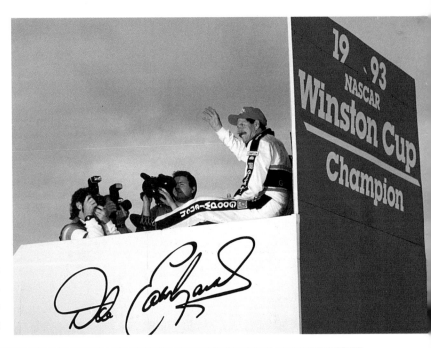

The crew of Dale Earnhardt's Goodwrench team hold up a banner proclaiming Dale the 1993 NASCAR Winston Cup Champion.

season in 1992, every person on our team made a conscious decision to find a way to perform better and to make the team work better.

It wasn't just me, or Richard Childress. Every single team member went and talked with Richard about what could be done and how it could be done, to make us competitive again.

Everyone reached down deeply inside himself, and rededicated himself to bringing Goodwrench Chevrolet back to the front of the pack. If it meant working more, or experimenting more, or switching jobs with another crew member, or whatever, they did it.

And right from the start, when we rolled off the truck in Daytona, I think people sensed that the 1993 season was not going to be a year like 1992. We were back, and we would stay that way throughout the year.

I can't say enough about the team and the work they did. The attitude was different this year. There was an air of confidence that was missing a

little bit last year — and there was also an attitude that "we're back — and we're going to be contenders any way we can through this season."

The team established a consistency early in the season that the crew guys continued throughout the season, race after race. We won some great races — the weekend at Charlotte was special, and we had a great Daytona, even if we didn't win the big race. It's kind of displeasing to us, in a way, that we didn't win a race the remainder of the year after Talladega in July, but it wasn't for lack of trying.

We were good — and competitive, but we ran into the Mark Martin buzzsaw in August and then Rusty's red-hot streak in the final third of the season. We had a few problems, but not many, and our consistency pulled us through Rusty's challenge and enabled us to win the Championship.

We had a new crew chief after Kirk Shelmerdine decided he wanted to leave and pursue his other dreams. Kirk's doing well in that respect now, and we were fortunate to have Andy Petree join us from Harry Gant's crew.

Andy made us believe in ourselves again, and worked hard to show the team leadership and gain the respect of the others on our team. It didn't take long for that to happen, and from the outset, Andy became a really important cog in our machine. Now, we get to take a "rookie" crew chief to New York and teach him how to party!

Although this season was filled with many great moments — like our victories, our battle with Rusty that brought out the best in both drivers and teams, and this championship — it also was one that will stay with me for a long time.

It was the year that we lost our Champion before he really had time to enjoy the title he worked so hard to win.

And it was the year that we lost another driver almost before we had gotten over the first loss.

During the 1992 season, I really grew to respect Alan Kulwicki because of what he accomplished. Alan and I hadn't had time to become the best of friends, but I had a lot of respect for him as a driver on the track — and as a car owner. He had made his greatest dreams come true by winning the Winston Cup — something that no one believed he ever would be able to do with his home-grown team.

I thought of his accomplishments in the same way that I take pride in what I've been able to do in racing. No one ever would have believed that I started racing in Charlotte, some small town kid from Kannapolis, and ever could have gotten to where I have been able to in this sport.

I was really proud of what Alan had accomplished — and I have the same pride in my team and myself. We both had been able to do things that people told us we couldn't; that no one but

Dale Earnhardt and Ricky Rudd take the field toward the green flag at Sears Point.

18

ourselves believed.

Then, to lose Davey Allison just a few weeks later was just as hard. I had a lot of respect for Davey as a driver, as a outdoor sportsman and as an Allison. We had hunted and fished together over the years, and I had gotten to know him better through Neil Bonnett.

Those things made it a season that had its valleys, along with its peaks.

Davey and Alan made Teresa and I talk about a lot of things, and think about a lot of things.

Sometimes, now, when things get all scheduled up, and all of the sudden it seems like there are not enough minutes in the day to do everything, I step back and look at things.

I think about the conversations Teresa and I had, and what we've thought about. I realize more and more that we should enjoy what we have, and be proud of what we have accomplished. We should spend as much time as we can with our loved ones, and be proud of them as people — as well as of their accomplishments.

In a lot of ways, I'm proud to be a kid from a small town. I'm proud of what I've been able to accomplish. Last year, Alan Kulwicki said that if what he had done was something that would inspire some to do better, to accomplish more than anyone expected of him, then he would feel he had made some impact.

I feel the same way. Alan did things his way, and I've been able to do a lot of things that many thought I'd never be able to accomplish.

Moving from dirt to asphalt racing· was one thing. Being able to get a ride in NASCAR Winston Cup was another. To become competitive enough to win a race was still another. Winning the first championship, when Cale Yarborough and Richard Petty were the big dogs and I was just a kid, was a huge accomplishment.

Then to win a second title, and a third, and a fourth and a fifth were all things that even I never thought I'd be able to accomplish.

Now we've won a sixth. Everyone already is talking about having a chance to tie Richard Pet-

ty's record with seven championships. I don't know if we will be able to do that. All I know is that we can try. We've gotten to the point, by working hard, believing in ourselves, and a little luck, where we can at least take a crack at winning a seventh title.

Whether we can do it or not, I don't know.

We'll begin the chase again in February.

Once the Championship week is over in New York, we'll begin focusing our attention on the 1994 season. We can't test until January 1, so that will give our team a well-deserved break during the month of December.

But February isn't far away.

I'll be trying to win that seventh championship in 1994.

But most importantly, I'm going to try my best —

Dale Earnhardt and Rusty Wallace
make a final tribute to Alan Kulwicki and Davey Allison.

and I'm sure our team will do the same — to win the race that still eludes me.

You can expect our best effort to win the Daytona 500.

In the meantime, let me close this by saying that no one appreciates the fans and the way they have supported our Goodwrench team more than Richard Childress and myself.

Whether we were winning or struggling, you stood behind us and supported us. We appreciate it, and during the 1994 season, we'll try to give you something more to cheer about.

Like a seventh NASCAR Winston Cup Championship.

1993

NASCAR WINSTON CUP CHAMPION

DALE EARNHARDT

The season began with high hopes for Rusty Wallace, Michael Waltrip and Dale Earnhardt. Only two of the three would battle for the championship at the end of the year.

Halfway through the NASCAR Winston Cup Awards Banquet in December, Dale Earnhardt was thinking about the nights that he was a guest of honor in the Waldorf-Astoria Hotel's Grand Ballroom.

Since 1986, the Awards Banquet had been a weekend spent in personal and team celebration for the Kannapolis, NC, native and the members of Richard Childress' team.

Four times during that span, he and his mates had been honored as the champions of their sport. The other two years, they had finished second or third after the long season. Twelve points had separated them from title-winner Rusty Wallace in 1989 or it would have been five Winston Cups during that span.

While Alan Kulwicki was being honored as the Champion, Earnhardt was planning for the future. He had finished 12th in the point standings and his only trip to the stage was to accept membership in the McDonald's All-Star Race team. It was

"The Other Dale" emerged from a late-race struggle to post the first-ever Daytona 500 by STP victory for the Jarrett family.

the first time since 1982 that Earnhardt failed to finish in the top-10 in the standings—and only the second time in his NASCAR Winston Cup career. Even in 1979, when he won the Rookie of the Year title, he finished seventh in the final point standings.

One thing was very clear in Earnhardt's mind that December evening in New York City. The 1993 season would not mirror the frustrations of 1992. The entire group from Childress' shop in Welcome, NC, was determined to return to the front of the ranks.

When Earnhardt's Goodwrench Chevrolet arrived at Daytona for Speedweeks, it took about three seconds for the garage denizens to figure out what was happening with the team. The air of confidence, lost somewhere in the early part of the 1992 season and never regained, had returned.

"Back in Black" was the theme of the team from Welcome. And the group, led by crew chief Andy Petree (recruited during the off-season from Harry Gant's Skoal effort) immediately began strutting its stuff. From the moment the team unloaded, Earnhardt was a factor with which every other team would have to contend.

Earnhardt wasn't the only driver with high hopes as the teams prepared for the sport's "Super Bowl" to open the season.

Rusty Wallace had spent the off-season in preparation and the 1989 NASCAR Winston Cup Champion told the media in January he would be a contender for the title. He put his Miller Genuine Draft Pontiac team into an aerobic and fitness program he hoped would yield strong results in 1993. Wallace was not interested in finishing 13th in the point standings again.

Dale Jarrett entered Daytona in the second year of development with Joe Gibbs' Interstate Batteries team. He had been 18th the previous season, failing to win a race, and had posted just over $400,000 in winnings—good for only 20th on the list at the end of the year.

Hut Stricklin went to Daytona with stars in his eyes. He was the proud new driver of Junior Johnson's McDonald's Ford and harbored high hopes for the season. Sterling Marlin had moved to the Stavola Brothers, taking Raybestos with him, and Bobby Allison Motorsports had Jimmy Spencer behind the wheel.

Davey Allison, who watched his hopes for his first Winston Cup disappear at Atlanta last November, hoped to find his way to victory lane for the second-straight year in the Daytona 500, wheeling his trusty Havoline Ford from Robert Yates' shop.

Alan Kulwicki, after winning the Winston Cup in the closest race in the history of the award, was back to defend his title with his Hooters Thunderbird. Derrike Cope, who watched his Bob Whitcomb-owned team shut the doors just two weeks before the season-opener, was in Cale Yarborough's Ford with one-time sponsorship from Bojangles' restaurants.

And for the first time in more than three decades, Richard Petty would see the Daytona 500 by STP from pit road, with Rick Wilson behind the wheel of the number 44 STP Pontiac.

Despite the months of testing and preparation, every team in the garage area was forced to consider the strength of Earnhardt—particularly after he decimated the field in the Busch Clash, the opening event for the NASCAR Winston Cup cars during Speedweeks. In the draw for starting position, he pulled out "13," made a rueful face, and then blasted to the front of the 15-car pack to snatch the lead from Ernie Irvan on the sixth lap. He cruised at the point to the end of the first ten laps, despite knowing that if he was the leader at the break, he would start shotgun for the final ten laps.

It didn't matter. Starting 15th, it took him just five laps to move to the front again, and he pulled out a two-car-length victory, pocketing $60,000 in just 16 minutes of racing.

The rookie crop for 1993 was as heralded as any since the 1979 season—when Earnhardt, Harry Gant and Terry Labonte fought their way across the country in search of the crown.

The 1993 season would see Jeff Gordon and his DuPont Chevrolet battle with Bobby Labonte and his Maxwell House Fords, fielded by Bill Davis and wrenched by Tim Brewer and Kenny Wallace, in Felix Sabates' Dirt Devil Pontiacs, with Jeff Hammond calling the shots as crew chief.

Gordon came to Daytona looking for seat time—and ended up winning the first of the Gatorade Twins in a shocking display of maturity and power. Bill Elliott and Kyle Petty were on the

21-year-old's tail at the checkered, but neither had anything for the latest Hendrick Motorsports driver.

In the second Gatorade Twin, Earnhardt again showed he was to be taken seriously. He led 34 of the 50 laps and after an early battle with Ricky Rudd, he powered his way to the victory over a surprisingly strong Geoff Bodine, beating the Motorcraft Ford driver by a car-length.

Earnhardt further set the stage by winning his fourth-consecutive Goody's 300 Busch Grand National event, beating Ken Schrader by two car-lengths.

Finally, Sunday rolled around, and with a national audience watching on CBS-TV, the black Chevrolet rolled out to do battle.

Since arriving at Daytona, Earnhardt had heard the same question over and over. Could he finally win the biggest prize in the sport? Would his 15th try at winning the Daytona 500 by STP be the lucky one?

It appeared so, as he battled his way to the lead on the seventh lap, moving underneath Dale Jarrett. And, as the day wore on, his was the dominant car, leading 11 times for 107 of the 200 laps.

There were others, sure, but every time Earn-

The action at Daytona transpired in packs of drafting cars. Rookie Jeff Gordon and Ernie Irvan led Bill Elliott and Alan Kulwicki, among others, during the 500 by STP.

hardt would be dropped from the lead, the wily five-time champion would fight his way back to the point.

The final battle to the checkered flag began after Rusty Wallace's made-for-TV wreck. Wallace was uninjured, but he wrecked his Pontiac in a three-car backstretch incident.

Earnhardt emerged at the front of the pack for the restart, knowing the snarling pack in his mirror held some very strong machines—including those of Geoff Bodine, Jarrett and Gordon. Stricklin also was having a great debut in the Golden Arches machine.

Jarrett grabbed the lead after the green flew, held it briefly and then lost it when he drifted high in the fourth turn with 21 laps to go.

Earnhardt was at the point, and he looked ready to win.

With Gordon on his rear bumper and Jarrett third, it was a Chevrolet party. And as the laps clicked down, "the other" Dale was watching the rear of Earnhardt's Chevrolet begin to slide in the corners.

Although early in the race, Dale Jarrett leads Dale Earnhardt and Geoff Bodine in what would be the finishing order of the top three. Ernie Irvan, involved in an early-race wreck, finished 37th.

Knowing he had to get past Gordon to have a chance, Jarrett made his move, to the outside of the rookie, with two laps to go. A surprised Gordon was a touch slow to react to Jarrett's unorthodox move, and by the time he could counter, Jarrett had moved his Chevrolet to second.

There are few cars wider on the final laps of any race than Earnhardt's. And as the three-car train rushed to the line to take the white flag, Earnhardt maintained his slight lead.

"Dale was loose in turn three, and I jumped underneath him, getting alongside as we went into the final turn," Jarrett explained after the race.

The cars bumped as they came out of the final turn on the run to the white flag, and Jarrett wondered if he had made his move at the wrong time.

"Jeff (Gordon) had moved over behind Earnhardt and I had no help," Jarrett said of the pickle he was in as the cars headed into the final 2.5 miles.

"Geoff Bodine pulled in behind me and that was just the little bit of 'shove' I needed. I knew I could win when I jumped out of the second turn in the lead and was able to keep the lead down the backstretch, through the final turns and through the trioval to the checkered flag."

When it was over, Earnhardt once again had to make the trip to North Carolina without the victo-

ry he wanted most. He had a plane full of hardware, toting home the trophies from his three wins—but not the biggest one from Speedweeks.

Dale Jarrett, with proud father Ned calling the final lap from the CBS booth, had won *THE* race that had eluded his father throughout his career. It was, as Dale said in the winner's circle, a victory for the entire Jarrett family.

Behind Earnhardt, Bodine survived to finish third, with Stricklin just acing Gordon at the line for fourth. Mark Martin finished sixth in a solid run, with Morgan Shepherd bringing the Wood Brothers' Ford home seventh.

As his KingAir took off from Daytona's airport, Earnhardt settled back in his leather seat. He might not have won the race, but he had fired the first salvo of the 1993 war for the championship.

He had led the most laps and had established from the get-go that the Richard Childress team was back—and would be a prominent contender for the 1993 Winston Cup Championship.

Although he had one of the fastest cars in the field, Bill Elliott would have engine problems in his Budweiser Ford, starting the season with a dismal 39th.

And if the Daytona 500 by STP was any indication, Earnhardt wouldn't be sitting at a table on the floor of the Waldorf come December. He and his mates would be at the head table.

Fin. Pos.	Str. Pos.	Driver	Team	Fin. Pos.	Str. Pos.	Driver	Team
1	2	Dale Jarrett	Interstate Batteries Chevrolet	22	16	Phil Parsons	Manheim Auctions Chevrolet
2	4	Dale Earnhardt	GM Goodwrench Chevrolet	23	24	Kenny Wallace	Dirt Devil Pontiac
3	6	Geoff Bodine	Motorcraft Ford	24	17	Chad Little	Mayflower Transit Ford
4	18	Hut Stricklin	McDonald's Ford	25	29	Jimmy Horton	Active Trucking Chevrolet
5	3	Jeff Gordon	DuPont Auto Finishes Chevrolet	26	10	Alan Kulwicki	Hooters Ford
6	23	Mark Martin	Valvoline Ford	27	27	Bobby Hamilton	Country Time Ford
7	32	Morgan Shepherd	Citgo Ford	28	11	Davey Allison	Havoline Ford
8	7	Ken Schrader	Kodiak Chevrolet	29	35	Derrike Cope	Bojangles' Ford
9	14	Sterling Marlin	Raybestos Ford	30	12	Ricky Rudd	Tide Chevrolet
10	22	Wally Dallenbach	Keystone Beer Ford	31	1	Kyle Petty	Mello Yello Pontiac
11	19	Terry Labonte	Kellogg's Chevrolet	32	34	Rusty Wallace	Miller Genuine Draft Pontiac
12	31	Rick Mast	Skoal Classic Ford	33	41	Dave Marcis	STG/Wehre Chevrolet
13	30	Jimmy Spencer	Meineke Ford	34	15	Rick Wilson	STP Pontiac
14	13	Lake Speed	Purex Ford	35	9	Bobby Hillin	Heilig-Meyers Ford
15	33	Ted Musgrave	Jasper Engines Ford	36	40	Al Unser	Valvoline Chevrolet
16	28	Michael Waltrip	Pennzoil Pontiac	37	8	Ernie Irvan	Kodak Film Chevrolet
17	20	Brett Bodine	Quaker State Ford	38	36	Joe Ruttman	Fina Lube Ford
18	26	Darrell Waltrip	Western Auto Chevrolet	39	5	Bill Elliott	Budweiser Ford
19	39	Jim Sauter	Evinrude Ford	40	38	Jimmy Hensley	NAPA Ford
20	25	Bobby Labonte	Maxwell House Ford	41	21	Dick Trickle	Carolina Pottery Ford
21	37	Harry Gant	Skoal Bandit Chevrolet				

GOODWRENCH 500

After a week of savoring his Daytona triumph, Dale Jarrett headed for the North Carolina Sandhills in an effort to make it two straight victories to open the young season.

Jarrett shared the point lead with Dale Earnhardt (who led the most laps at Daytona), but knew that this was the Goodwrench-sponsored race at North Carolina Motor Speedway—and that Earnhardt would be pulling out the stops to try to win his sponsor's event.

Rusty Wallace had spent the ten days between Daytona and the opening of practice at Rockingham healing up the slight bruises he sustained in his late-race tumbling act at Daytona and knew he needed to have a strong run if he was to recover from the 113-point deficit he already carried in the point race.

Davey Allison and Alan Kulwicki found themselves chasing the leaders as well. Davey had finished 28th in the season-opener, three laps

Hut Stricklin's hopes for a great season in the Junior Johnson McDonald's Ford were bolstered by solid pit stops.

Bill Elliott, Ted Musgrave, Ken Schrader and Dale Earnhardt

receive pit-road attention from their crews.

behind, and Alan had opened defense of his title with a 26th-place finish at Daytona.

For the past few years, Rockingham had been kind to Kyle Petty, and the Mello Yello Pontiac driver headed for the tricky one-mile track knowing he needed something good to happen. He had been involved in the multi-car wreck on Daytona's front-stretch, and ended up classified 31st in the race results. He was 105 points behind "the Dales" after the first race.

Bojangles', delighted with Derrike Cope's performance at Daytona (he led three times for 30 laps), stepped into the NASCAR Winston Cup wars with an announcement of sponsorship of Cale Yarborough's team for the remainder of the season. Without a ride two weeks before the Daytona 500 by STP, Cope now was assured of having a competitive car for the remainder of the season.

Kyle had won four-straight pole positions (and five of the last six) at Rockingham, and everyone expected the green and black Pontiac to be at the point again.

Surprise, surprise!

Mark Martin, who said afterward that he didn't

expect his lap to be good enough for the pole, found out it was when the qualifying session was over. He bested Ernie Irvan and Bill Elliott, with surprising Rick Mast and Ted Musgrave fourth- and fifth-fastest.

Where was Kyle?

His lap was only good enough for 11th, nearly a mile per hour slower than Martin.

Cope responded to the sponsorship announcement by qualifying ninth, while Rusty would start tenth for the Sunday race.

Earnhardt would start seventh and co-point leader Jarrett would take the green flag from the 22nd place on the grid.

The first half of the four-hour event saw Earnhardt, Irvan and Martin establish themselves as the front-runners, with Geoff Bodine, Darrell Waltrip and Ted Musgrave taking the lead during green flag pit stops.

Rusty came to the front for the first time at lap 275 and began showing the strength he had claimed his Miller Pontiac possessed throughout the weekend.

His car was one of the best in the field, no

Brett Bodine served notice that he would be strong in 1993 when he battled Rusty Wallace for position at Rockingham.

When the green flag fell, pole-sitter Mark Martin led Ernie Irvan and the rest of the field at the start of the 492-lap journey.

doubt. But it was this race in which Wallace's crew would begin to show the NASCAR Winston Cup world the results of the three months of conditioning exercises the team members had been undergoing at the shop.

During each of the final three caution flags, Wallace's crew put him out of his stall first, and the Missouri native took advantage of their speed.

"The pit stops were so dog-gone fast it was unreal," Wallace would say afterward. "It seemed that just as soon as the car was jacked up, it was going back down. I hardly had time to get a drink before it was time to go."

And when it was time to go, that's exactly what Wallace did. In the final 25 laps, he watched his lead over Earnhardt and Irvan shrink to just a half-second, but that was more than enough to bring Wallace his 22nd career victory.

Harry Gant looked like a sure contender until an oil-belt problem surfaced with just 40 laps to go. Davey Allison was involved in a spin after being tagged by Bill Elliott and finished 14th. Pole-sitter Mark Martin finished fifth with a solid run

and Dale Jarrett came home sixth, his best-ever finish at Rockingham.

Phil Parsons posted the first top-10 finish in the history of Hendrick Motorsports, bringing the Manheim Auctions Chevrolet home eighth, the final car on the lead lap.

Defending NASCAR Winston Cup champion Alan Kulwicki finished the race in fourth place.

And what about Kyle?

One of the race favorites, the third-generation driver had a long race right from the beginning. On his first pit stop, he lost the clutch on his Pontiac and spent time in the garage area while his crew replaced it. He returned to the track and was able to make up three laps, proving his car was one of the strongest in the field, but he was classified 32nd at the end of the race, 62 laps behind the winner.

Earnhardt's second place boosted him into a 25-point lead over Jarrett as the teams began preparations for the first short-track race of the season at Richmond, VA. Geoff Bodine used his ninth-place finish at Rockingham to vault into third place in the standings, 42 points behind Earnhardt. Mark Martin was fourth in the points, with Hut Stricklin fifth after his 13th-place Rockingham finish.

Bill Elliott and Ricky Rudd staged a battle for 11th place at Rockingham. Elliott won the struggle.

Terry Labonte and Bobby Hillin battle for position in the North Carolina Sandhills. Labonte would notch his first top-10 finish of the season for the Kellogg's Chevrolet.

After leading much of the race, Rusty Wallace gained his first victory of the year in the Goodwrench 500, beating Dale Earnhardt by a half-second.

Fin. Pos.	Str. Pos.	Driver	Team	Fin. Pos.	Str. Pos.	Driver	Team
1	10	Rusty Wallace	Miller Genuine Draft Pontiac	21	40	Dave Marcis	STG Chevrolet
2	7	Dale Earnhardt	GM Goodwrench Chevrolet	22	6	Brett Bodine	Quaker State Ford
3	2	Ernie Irvan	Kodak Film Chevrolet	23	32	Kenny Wallace	Dirt Devil Pontiac
4	20	Alan Kulwicki	Hooters Ford	24	13	Ken Schrader	Kodiak Chevrolet
5	1	Mark Martin	Valvoline Ford	25	34	Jimmy Hensley	Hurley Limo Ford
6	22	Dale Jarrett	Interstate Batteries Chevrolet	26	30	Michael Waltrip	Pennzoil Pontiac
7	5	Ted Musgrave	Jasper Engines Ford	27	33	Ed Ferree	Cars & Credit Chevrolet
8	17	Phil Parsons	Manheim Auctions Chevrolet	28	19	Sterling Marlin	Raybestos Brakes Ford
9	14	Geoff Bodine	Motorcraft Ford	29	31	Dick Trickle	Carolina Pottery Ford
10	21	Terry Labonte	Kellogg's Chevrolet	30	27	Darrell Waltrip	Western Auto Chevrolet
11	3	Bill Elliott	Budweiser Ford	31	26	Harry Gant	Skoal Bandit Chevrolet
12	12	Ricky Rudd	Tide Chevrolet	32	11	Kyle Petty	Mello Yello Pontiac
13	8	Hut Stricklin	McDonald's Ford	33	24	Bobby Labonte	Maxwell House Ford
14	39	Davey Allison	Havoline Ford	34	28	Jeff Gordon	DuPont Auto Finishes Chevrolet
15	23	Bobby Hamilton	Country Time Ford	35	16	Morgan Shepherd	Citgo Ford
16	25	Jimmy Spencer	Meineke Ford	36	35	John Chapman	Bahre Racing Pontiac
17	15	Rick Wilson	STP Pontiac	37	36	Mike Potter	Kenova Construction Ford
18	9	Derrike Cope	Bojangles' Ford	38	37	Jerry Hill	Bell Motor Company Chevrolet
19	18	Bobby Hillin	Heilig-Meyers Ford	39	4	Rick Mast	Servco-Skoal Classic Ford
20	29	Wally Dallenbach	Keystone Beer Ford	40	38	James Hylton	Rumple Pontiac

PONTIAC EXCITEMENT 400

There's not a bad seat anywhere in the Richmond house when it comes time for NASCAR Winston Cup racing.

Richmond's annual spring get-together usually signals the settling-in of teams—not changes this early in the NASCAR Winston Cup season.

But one of the news flashes of the first short-track weekend of the year was that Waddell Wilson, head of the research and development team at Hendrick Motorsports, would begin work the following Monday as the General Manager of Larry Hedrick's team, fielding Chevrolets for Phil Parsons.

And the second piece of news was the absence of Junior Johnson, who was at Duke University Medical Center, recuperating from successful elective heart surgery.

Richard Petty continued to make the adjustment from driver to car owner at Richmond.

Ken Schrader proved to be the surprise of qualifying, notching his first short-track pole after 11 other poles won during his career on super-speedways. He attributed his fast Richmond lap to new Goodyear Eagle radial tires, used to eliminate Davey Allison's old record, set in September 1988 on Goodyear bias-plies.

Rick Mast continued his string of excellent qualifying runs with an outside pole, while Morgan Shepherd put the Wood Brothers' Citgo Ford on the inside of the second row, alongside Brett Bodine's Quaker State Ford, powered by Ernie Elliott motors again this year.

Darrell Waltrip and Alan Kulwicki were lined up in the third row while Kyle Petty and Jeff Gordon would make up the fourth row ahead of Dale Jarrett and Ernie Irvan. Point-leader Dale Earnhardt would be 11th for the Sunday start.

Geoff Bodine was missing from qualifying after backing his Motorcraft Ford into the fourth turn wall during the first of his two laps. He was unable to post a time, and the team pulled the back-up Ford off the red truck. Bodine would return in second-round qualifying to post the fastest lap and claim the Busch award.

While the hotshots at the front of the field were figuring strategy, Davey Allison and his Robert Yates teammates kept working on their black Thunderbird. Allison had qualified 14th—and al-though the team didn't feel they were totally out at the lunch counter, they knew they still had to find the handle to make Allison competitive.

The last time the team had won was at Phoenix the previous November—and although the losing streak numbered just three races coming into Richmond, it had actually been five months since the group had tasted the sweet nectar of victory champagne.

Schrader jumped to the lead from the start, soon to be displaced by Morgan Shepherd and then by a sweet-running Darrell Waltrip.

Waltrip and Kyle Petty battled for the lead for more than 110 laps, with Kyle putting the Mello Yello Pontiac at the point for over a quarter of the 400-lap distance.

Allison, meanwhile, had picked his way toward the front of the field, helped by a quick pit stop by his crew that boosted him to second place near the mid-point when a yellow flew after pole-sitter Schrader slapped the second turn wall.

The third (and surprisingly, final) caution of the race was the one that turned the race around for Allison. With just over 150 laps remaining in the race, the yellow flew for oil in the third turn and Allison's crew responded with an 18.21-second, four-tire stop that put Davey back on the track first, and at the point for the restart.

In turn, Davey went to work to protect the lead his team had worked so hard on pit road to give him. He led the race for the next 110 laps until he made his final stop under green with only 47 laps

Defending Winston Cup Champion Alan Kulwicki backed up his Rockingham fourth with a rock-solid third at Richmond to move from ninth to sixth in the point standings.

remaining in the race.

With the lead on the line, once again his "patches"-clad crew responded, taking only 17.36 for four tires and a single can of Unocal.

After the green-flag stops cycled around, Allison was back at the point and was never challenged. He coasted to a four-second victory over Rusty Wallace and after the race, crew chief Larry McReynolds explained the last stop.

"We only needed one can of gas—because that's all we needed to go the remainder of the race," McReynolds said. "Because of that, it let us use more people to help change the tires—and we got out of the pits that much faster."

For Allison, the victory was the 19th of his career, and he felt throughout the race that if he could get to the front of the field, he had the car he needed to win.

"I felt that our car, the 2 (Rusty) and the 42 (Kyle) were all about equal—and that if I could get to the lead, whether it was by passing on the track or by pit stops, we would be able to stay at the front," Davey said after his win.

"Then we had that pit stop that put us out front and I felt like all we had to do from that point on was not mess up on the race track, not

Rick Mast, after qualifying second-fastest, saw his hopes for his first Winston Cup victory go up in smoke with engine problems.

He qualified only 14th, but came through the field to win in runaway style. The victory was the 19th of Davey Allison's career, moving him into a tie with Fonty Flock and Buddy Baker for 24th on the all-time list.

abuse the race car, take care of it—and we would be okay by the end of the race."

Part of Davey's optimism about Sunday's race and the way his Ford would perform came Saturday evening when he attended mass at St. John's church in Richmond.

"I was just sitting there with my cousin Tommy (Allison) and Larry (McReynolds) when all of a sudden I started getting chills," Davey said. "I wasn't thinking about anything in particular, just trying to pay attention to what was going on in mass.

"All of a sudden, I started getting goose

bumps. This morning I woke up and I was wide-open. I felt like I was spring-loaded this morning."

The good feelings Davey carried into the race, and his first victory after two dismal season-opening races, helped vault the Ford driver to eighth in the point standings, a major jump from the 18th place he occupied prior to the start of the Richmond event.

While the eyes of the huge crowd were on Allison, "Slider" was beginning to work his magic.

Alan Kulwicki may not have led a lap in the Richmond race, but he moved through the field to a third-place finish behind Wallace, posting his second consecutive top-five finish and moving to

sixth in the point standings.

Dale Jarrett finished fourth in the event, and coupled with Dale Earnhardt's tenth-place finish, moved into the point lead by a single digit after three races.

Earnhardt appeared headed for at least another top-five finish when he was hit with a 15-second penalty by NASCAR after he was caught speeding on pit road for his final pit stop with 50 laps to go.

The penalty cost Earnhardt a lap, and he was classified 10th at the end of the event.

Kyle Petty finished a solid fifth, but Bill Elliott had another dismal showing for Junior Johnson's Budweiser Ford team. Engine problems sidelined him for the second time in three races.

Rookie sensation Jeff Gordon was sixth at the end of the race, posting his second top-10 of the season, while Darrell Waltrip had one of his better runs since Darlington the previous September, finishing just behind Mark Martin. Harry Gant was the final car on the lead lap, finishing ninth.

Martin's third-straight top-10 moved him into third place in the standings, 34 points behind Jarrett. Geoff Bodine was fourth, with Rusty Wallace fifth in the point battle.

Richmond in March can make even the hardiest bundle up.

There's plenty of room for the crew to work on Richmond's pit road. Davey Allison heads for his pit, while Ernie Irvan and Jeff Gordon get service.

Davey Allison and his entire group share the excitement of their first victory of the season in the winner's circle.

Fin. Pos.	Str. Pos.	Driver	Team	Fin. Pos.	Str. Pos.	Driver	Team
1	14	Davey Allison	Havoline Ford	19	17	Derrike Cope	Bojangles' Ford
2	13	Rusty Wallace	Miller Genuine Draft Pontiac	20	1	Ken Schrader	Kodiak Chevrolet
3	6	Alan Kulwicki	Hooters Ford	21	27	Dick Trickle	Carolina Pottery Ford
4	9	Dale Jarrett	Interstate Batteries Chevrolet	22	35	Bobby Hamilton	Country Time Ford
5	7	Kyle Petty	Mello Yello Pontiac	23	26	Michael Waltrip	Pennzoil Pontiac
6	8	Jeff Gordon	DuPont Auto Finishes Chevrolet	24	19	Terry Labonte	Kellogg's Chevrolet
7	12	Mark Martin	Valvoline Ford	25	18	Rick Wilson	STP Pontiac
8	5	Darrell Waltrip	Western Auto Chevrolet	26	32	Kenny Wallace	Dirt Devil Pontiac
9	34	Harry Gant	Skoal Bandit Chevrolet	27	22	Wally Dallenbach	Keystone Beer Ford
10	11	Dale Earnhardt	GM Goodwrench Chevrolet	28	30	Bobby Hillin	Heilig-Meyers Ford
11	10	Ernie Irvan	Kodak Film Chevrolet	29	20	Bobby Labonte	Maxwell House Ford
12	21	Geoff Bodine	Motorcraft Ford	30	31	Lake Speed	Purex Ford
13	24	Jimmy Spencer	Meineke Ford	31	23	Sterling Marlin	Raybestos Brakes Ford
14	3	Morgan Shepherd	Citgo Ford	32	4	Brett Bodine	Quaker State Ford
15	15	Ricky Rudd	Tide Chevrolet	33	25	Bill Elliott	Budweiser Ford
16	28	Phil Parsons	Manheim Auctions Chevrolet	34	36	Jimmy Hensley	Hurley Limo Ford
17	16	Ted Musgrave	Jasper Engines Ford	35	2	Rick Mast	Skoal Classic Ford
18	33	Hut Stricklin	McDonald's Ford	36	29	Dave Marcis	STG Chevrolet

MOTORCRAFT QUALITY PARTS 500

**ATLANTA MOTOR
SPEEDWAY**

MARCH 20, 1993

From time to time, it becomes apparent that Mother Nature isn't interested in watching a race the day it's scheduled. This time, it was Atlanta Motor Speedway's turn to reschedule, after a blizzard paralyzed the east coast, sending the Winston Cuppers home only to return the following Saturday. Rain began right after Rusty Wallace led the first round of qualifying Friday afternoon at Bruton Smith's 1.5 mile track, and overnight, the rain turned to snow. By the time NASCAR called the race at approximately noon Saturday, one of the busiest airports in the world was closed. And when the storm was finished, some 450,000 people in the Atlanta area were without power.

Race fans and teams were stranded in hotel rooms in the area, and the National Guard was called out for assistance. After the snow slacked off, freezing rain coated everything and as the temperature plummeted in the afternoon, winds in excess of 50 miles per hour took the wind-chill factor to more than 11 degrees below zero.

Jeff Gordon's hopes for a win ended with a late-race pit stop for fuel. He finished fourth, one lap in arrears.

Stretching his fuel to the max, Morgan Shepherd celebrated his victory in Atlanta's winner's circle.

The "Blizzard of '93" brought an end to the hopes of running the Motorcraft 500 on its appointed day.

The cars were impounded in the AMS garage area, and when the teams returned to the track the following weekend, crews were allowed to work feverishly on their mounts before the race began.

Wallace would start from the pole, with Dale Earnhardt alongside. The two black GM machines headed Mark Martin and Jeff Gordon, with Ernie Irvan and Brett Bodine forming the third row of the grid. Morgan Shepherd and Terry Labonte occupied the fourth row, ahead of Ted Musgrave and Kenny Schrader.

Derrike Cope would start 11th, while Dick Trickle had the best qualifying effort of the young season for the Carolina Pottery-sponsored Rah-Moc Ford.

Because second-round qualifying was canceled by the snowstorm, the entire field was determined by the single qualifying session the week before. Greg Sacks and James Hylton made the slowest timed runs in the first session while Rich Bickle and Rick Crawford did not make first-round qualifying runs. Bickle damaged his car during practice and did not have a second car.

Among those who would start toward the rear of the field due to poor first-round qualifying efforts were Richmond winner Davey Allison (31st), and front-runners Dale Jarrett (33rd) and Alan Kulwicki (29th).

When the green flag finally dropped to start the Motorcraft 500, Rusty Wallace and Mark Martin wasted no time showing they had their cars dialed in for the Atlanta track.

The two traded the lead for the first 60 laps before the teams started cycling through green flag pit stops. During that period, Ken Schrader, Geoff Bodine and Wally Dallenbach briefly held the lead, with the race returning to a battle between Wallace and Martin after the green flag stops were over.

After half-distance, Martin had firmly established his Valvoline Ford as the dominant car, having led for 140 of the 225 laps. But then Martin's hopes for his first victory of the season ended when he made the hard left-hand turn into the garage area with something broken in the bottom end of the motor.

When Martin made his garage call, it looked like Wallace might be home free for his second victory of the season. But two laps later, Morgan Shepherd swept past the black Pontiac to lead for the next 29 laps.

Then, Shepherd's dreams for his first win since 1990 appeared to disappear.

With a cut tire exiting the fourth turn, Shepherd limped all the way around the track to stop for tires and fuel on lap 260.

But the other leaders had to pit under green as well, and the economy run began.

As the laps wound down, Wallace made his stop for gas on lap 302 of the 328-lap race. Jeff Gordon became the leader—but had to make his stop 12 laps from the end of the race. The only drivers who had not pitted were Ernie Irvan—and Shepherd.

With seven laps left, Morgan had a 19-second lead over the Kodak Chevrolet—but Eddie Wood had made the decision regarding Morgan's attempt to win long before that.

With 30 laps to go, Eddie radioed Morgan to start saving fuel in hopes of stretching what they had in the tank to make it to the end of the race.

"I started easing out of the throttle before I got to the corner, and instead of jumping on the gas when I came off the corner, I just eased it out and tried not to use too much accelerator," Shepherd said after the race.

"My heart really dropped to my stomach when the tire went down," Shepherd added. "But I learned never to give up a long time ago. Although our hopes seemed gone, I just kept plugging away."

Shepherd said he didn't believe he had won when the checkered flag fell for him at the end. Wallace didn't believe it either, because he was not aware that neither Shepherd nor Irvan had made a final stop.

Pit road proved to be the place where the Motorcraft 500 was won—and lost.

Gordon's hopes for his first victory ended when he slapped the wall after his final, gas-only pit stop. He admitted he had made a couple of "rookie" mistakes that may have cost him a chance for the win. He overshot his pit on the final stop, had to have his crew push him back into the pit stall before they could service his car—and then let the car slap the wall.

Irvan finished second—his best performance of the young season—ahead of Wallace. Those three were the only drivers on the lead lap.

Gordon was fourth, while Ricky Rudd, Geoff Bodine (battling the flu) and Kyle Petty battled their way to fifth, sixth and seventh place finishes. Brett Bodine was eighth, the last car a lap down—and Bill Elliott struggled at his home track.

Elliott was classified ninth, but was two laps in arrears in the Budweiser Ford.

Dale Earnhardt finished 11th while Davey Allison was 13th. While Earnhardt was grinding out his finish, Dale Jarrett fell from the Winston Cup point lead after returning to action following a wreck. Jarrett emerged 31st in the race and fell to fourth in the point standings.

Earnhardt moved back into the point lead, with Geoff Bodine moving up to the runner-up position, just 19 markers behind the black Chevrolet driver. Wallace was now third in the standings, eight points behind Bodine, while Jeff Gordon climbed to fifth in the standings.

Mark Martin was sixth and Ernie Irvan had climbed to seventh, just ahead of race-winner Shepherd. Davey Allison now stood ninth in the standings, 110 points behind Earnhardt.

Last November, Atlanta had been the site of Alan Kulwicki's most glorious moment—the track where he was crowned Winston Cup champion. This day, however, Alan was classified 36th after he tangled with Dick Trickle in an early-race accident. Alan was now 14th in the standings after the first four races of the young season.

Rusty Wallace looked set to win his second race of the year, but Morgan's fuel gamble put Wallace in third at the end.

Crew members fought the elements to get gear packed up for the six-day race delay.

Fin. Pos.	Str. Pos.	Driver	Team	Fin. Pos.	Str. Pos.	Driver	Team
1	7	Morgan Shepherd	Citgo Ford	21	16	Harry Gant	Skoal Bandit Chevrolet
2	5	Ernie Irvan	Kodak Film Chevrolet	22	37	Jimmy Means	Hurley Limo Ford
3	1	Rusty Wallace	Miller Genuine Draft Pontiac	23	40	Greg Sacks	Melling Ford
4	4	Jeff Gordon	DuPont Auto Finishes Chevrolet	24	24	Rick Wilson	STP Pontiac
5	14	Ricky Rudd	Tide Chevrolet	25	36	Wally Dallenbach	Keystone Beer Ford
6	21	Geoff Bodine	Motorcraft Ford	26	23	Bobby Hamilton	Country Time Ford
7	27	Kyle Petty	Mello Yello Pontiac	27	32	Jimmy Horton	Active Trucking Chevrolet
8	6	Brett Bodine	Quaker State Ford	28	28	Lake Speed	Purex Ford
9	15	Bill Elliott	Budweiser Ford	29	10	Ken Schrader	Kodiak Chevrolet
10	18	Jimmy Spencer	Meineke Mufflers Ford	30	13	Rick Mast	Skoal Classic Ford
11	2	Dale Earnhardt	GM Goodwrench Chevrolet	31	33	Dale Jarrett	Interstate Batteries Chevrolet
12	20	Sterling Marlin	Raybestos Ford	32	3	Mark Martin	Valvoline Ford
13	31	Davey Allison	Havoline Ford	33	8	Terry Labonte	Kellogg's Chevrolet
14	22	Michael Waltrip	Pennzoil Pontiac	34	38	Dave Marcis	STG Chevrolet
15	19	Bobby Hillin	Heilig-Meyers Ford	35	35	Darrell Waltrip	Western Auto Chevrolet
16	26	Kenny Wallace	Dirt Devil Pontiac	36	29	Alan Kulwicki	Hooters Ford
17	11	Derrike Cope	Bojangles' Ford	37	12	Dick Trickle	Carolina Pottery Ford
18	17	Bobby Labonte	Maxwell House Ford	38	30	Joe Ruttman	Fina Lube Ford
19	9	Ted Musgrave	Jasper Engines Ford	39	25	Phil Parsons	Manheim Auctions Chevrolet
20	34	Hut Stricklin	McDonald's Ford	40	39	Bob Schacht	Pronto Auto Parts Oldsmobile

TRANSOUTH FINANCIAL 500

Another strong finish by defending champion Alan Kulwicki (sixth) fueled his team's hopes for a second-straight Winston Cup title.

When a driver has won 53 times in his career and had been as close to the front in every race of the early season as Dale Earnhardt had been, it was surprising to remember that the last time the Chevrolet driver had visited Victory Lane was last May at Charlotte in the Coca-Cola 600.

Yet, it had been 23 races since Earnhardt's last win—more than enough to make everyone understand why the proud driver had dedicated this season to returning to the front of the pack on a race-to-race basis.

Earnhardt had done that, and moved into friendly (to him, anyway!) Darlington Raceway for the TranSouth Financial 500 on the top of the ladder of the NASCAR Winston Cup Series point list.

Jeff Gordon started fifth, but soon became all too familiar with Darlington's finicky ways.

Atlanta winner Morgan Shepherd notched another top-10 finish at Darlington, after quick work on pit road by the Wood Brothers.

Over the years, Earnhardt had always treated Darlington with respect—and the few times he had tried to take advantage of the track, he was smartly slapped right in the kisser. Those few lessons had been learned well and the track had rewarded him mightily.

Few drivers have the record Earnhardt has compiled at Darlington, where only five drivers have won five or more times in their careers.

Darrell Waltrip, Bobby Allison and Cale Yarborough each have five trophies from Darlington races. David Pearson is the acknowledged master of the track "too tough to tame" with ten career victories. And Dale Earnhardt is somewhere in the middle of those, with seven victories—four coming in the TranSouth 500 in the spring.

It wasn't difficult, then, to understand the smile on Earnhardt's face as the black transporter discharged his Goodwrench Chevrolet for the fifth race of the season.

Despite all his success at Darlington, Earnhardt had only qualified for the pole once—when he was the fastest qualifier for the 1990 Southern 500.

Determined to start the race from the front, Dale cranked the fastest practice lap, well under Sterling Marlin's event record from last year—but never got a chance to show what he could do in qualifying.

Rain washed out the qualifying sessions—but Dale would be able to start from the pole, after all. The starting order was determined by the point standings—and Dale was one point ahead of Geoff Bodine after the first four races of the season.

Lining up behind the black Chevrolet and the red Ford were Rusty Wallace and Dale Jarrett, with rookie Jeff Gordon and Mark Martin making up the third row. Ernie Irvan, Morgan Shepherd, Davey Allison and Hut Stricklin completed the top ten.

The rain proved to be a stroke of luck for Gordon and fellow rookies Kenny Wallace and Bobby Labonte.

Traditionally, rookies aren't permitted to qualify in the first round of trials at Darlington. Candidates must first complete and pass a rookie test, given on the morning of the second round of qualifying. Then they can compete for a spot in the second half of the field.

But because of the rain, Gordon would start fifth in Sunday's race.

Geoff Bodine moved past Earnhardt early in the going, but Dale went to the point at the 50-lap mark. Then Mark Martin proved his Valvoline Ford was dialed in on the tricky track and he became Earnhardt's main competition. Mark swept past and Dale headed for pit road for a green-flag stop on lap 99, losing a lap in the process. A lap later, Gordon tagged the first-turn wall, bringing out the first yellow. As everyone pitted, Earnhardt found himself on the tail end of the lead lap—and hope as he might for a second yellow, he would have to wait 78 laps for the next caution and the chance to get his lap back.

While Earnhardt was fighting to stay on the tail of the lead lap, Martin simply streaked out to the lead. His Ford was as good as it could be, and he dominated the mid-portion of the event.

After that second yellow, Earnhardt lined up tenth for the restart, and it didn't take the Kannapolis, NC, native long to start making his moves to the front.

Within 20 laps, he was third. Two laps later he was second but trailed Martin by six seconds.

The third, and final, yellow of the race came when Bobby Labonte spun and Jimmy Spencer hit the wall on lap 215.

The leaders hit pit road and Earnhardt's "Flying Aces" did their work to perfection. He was the first one back on the track, and led the remainder of the race, except when he made his final green-flag stop for tires and fuel.

"We were on the money and as good as anyone could ask for," Martin ruefully shook his head after the race. "Dale was just simply exceptional during the final half of the race. The first half, I felt like we could do something with him—and we did.

"But his crew got his car better and better and at the end, we didn't have anything that we could do with him."

After the final stops, Earnhardt's lead was more than five seconds—and after he realized that Mark had no chance at him, the five-time champion eased up.

"I ran hard until about 20 laps to go and I saw that Mark was more than a half of a straightaway behind me," Earnhardt said. "Then I just tried to be consistent. I tried not to spin the tires and be rough on them, because if Mark was about to catch me, I wanted something left on the tires to

Ernie Irvan's Kodak crew worked hard to get him a good finish, but overheating sent the Chevrolet to 22nd place at the end of the event.

Geoff Bodine and Dale Earnhardt had a furious battle early in the race. Dale went on to win, and Geoff posted an eighth-place finish.

use, if I had to."

Earnhardt's victory enabled him to tie Lee Petty for sixth on the all-time career victory list with 54. And it made him an eight-time winner at Darlington, closing the gap on David Pearson.

"It's pretty neat to catch or get close," Earnhardt said when told of his accomplishments. "I'm two championships behind Richard and I'm two races behind David and those are drivers

Mark Martin's pit crew helped him to a second-place finish at venerable Darlington.

I have admired and looked up to all my career. It's pretty neat to be able to tie Lee on the win list, because he was one of the pioneers of the sport, and Richard and I are second-generation drivers. It's real special to be able to accomplish so much in this sport."

The only other two cars on the lead lap at the finish were Dale Jarrett and Ken Schrader, while Rusty Wallace was fifth, ahead of a furious battle between Alan Kulwicki and Kyle Petty for sixth

place. Geoff Bodine and Terry Labonte finished eighth and ninth.

Morgan Shepherd and Davey Allison were tenth and 11th.

Earnhardt's victory, complete with the five-point bonus for leading the most laps in the race, moved him into a 57-point lead over Geoff Bodine and Wallace as the teams loaded to leave Darlington. Dale Jarrett was fourth in the standings, while Mark Martin had moved to fifth, just ahead of a tie between Davey Allison and Morgan Shepherd. Jeff Gordon was eighth in the standings.

After the 36th place at Atlanta, Kulwicki was back on track. His sixth place in Darlington, combined with his fourth place at Rockingham and a third at Richmond, had countered his 26th at Daytona and the Atlanta finish. He emerged from the first five races ninth in the standings, 179 points behind Earnhardt—but was headed for the tracks where he annually posted solid finishes.

Bristol was next, and Alan was grinning when reminded he had won the April event there the previous year. "We did the best we could here at Darlington this week. We were about a fifth-place car and we finished sixth," Kulwicki said.

"You've got to be smart and run the best with what you've got that day. There will be another day when we'll be better."

Dale Earnhardt, wife Teresa and daughter Taylor celebrated his Darlington victory. Dale became the fifth-different driver to win in the first five races of the season.

Fin. Pos.	Str. Pos.	Driver	Team	Fin. Pos.	Str. Pos.	Driver	Team
1	1	Dale Earnhardt	GM Goodwrench Chevrolet	21	18	Sterling Marlin	Raybestos Brakes Ford
2	6	Mark Martin	Valvoline Ford	22	7	Ernie Irvan	Kodak Film Chevrolet
3	4	Dale Jarrett	Interstate Batteries Chevrolet	23	27	Bobby Hamilton	Country Time Ford
4	16	Ken Schrader	Kodiak Chevrolet	24	5	Jeff Gordon	DuPont Auto Finishes Chevrolet
5	3	Rusty Wallace	Miller Genuine Draft Pontiac	25	34	Dave Marcis	1-900-73-Races Chevrolet
6	14	Alan Kulwicki	Hooters Ford	26	30	Rick Wilson	STP Pontiac
7	15	Kyle Petty	Mello Yello Pontiac	27	35	Bob Schacht	Pronto Auto Parts Oldsmobile
8	2	Geoff Bodine	Motorcraft Ford	28	10	Hut Stricklin	McDonald's Ford
9	17	Terry Labonte	Kellogg's Chevrolet	29	11	Jimmy Spencer	Meineke Mufflers Ford
10	8	Morgan Shepherd	Citgo Ford	30	12	Ted Musgrave	Jasper Engines Ford
11	9	Davey Allison	Havoline Ford	31	33	Jimmy Means	Hurley Limo Ford
12	19	Brett Bodine	Quaker State Ford	32	26	Kenny Wallace	Dirt Devil Pontiac
13	22	Wally Dallenbach	Keystone Beer Ford	33	21	Michael Waltrip	Pennzoil Pontiac
14	28	Bill Elliott	Budweiser Ford	34	37	James Hylton	Rumple Furniture Pontiac
15	31	Rick Mast	Skoal Classic Ford	35	29	Bobby Hillin	Heilig-Meyers Ford
16	25	Darrell Waltrip	Western Auto Chevrolet	36	24	Phil Parsons	Manheim Auctions Chevrolet
17	23	Derrike Cope	Bojangles' Ford	37	20	Harry Gant	Skoal Bandit Chevrolet
18	36	Bobby Labonte	Maxwell House Ford	38	38	Mike Potter	Hurley Limo Ford
19	13	Ricky Rudd	Tide Chevrolet	39	39	Norm Benning	O'Neal Racing Oldsmobile
20	32	Dick Trickle	Carolina Pottery Ford				

FOOD CITY 500

The Wood Brothers worked hard on pit road to bring Morgan Shepherd yet another top-10 finish at Bristol.

O n the eve of practice, team members were checking into Bristol area hotels, having a bite to eat, or watching television in preparation for turning in prior to Friday morning's opening of practice for the Food City 500 at Larry Carrier's steeply-banked half-miler in Thunder Valley.

At the same time, the sport of NASCAR Winston Cup racing received a blow when defending champion Alan Kulwicki perished near the Bristol airport when the private plane he was aboard crashed.

Kulwicki had completed a personal appearance for sponsor Hooters in nearby Knoxville and was headed for Bristol. On board the Hooters corporate plane with him were Mark Brooks, the firm's sports marketing manager and son of Hooters of America Chairman Robert H. Brooks; Dan Duncan, Hooters' director of sports management and

Rusty dedicated his second victory of the year to his Midwest running-mate, Alan Kulwicki.

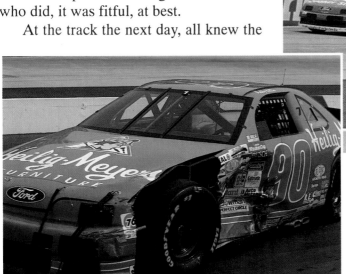

Another sell-out crowd was packed into Larry Carrier's awesome half-mile in Thunder Valley.

corporate pilot Charlie Campbell.

The Hooters twin-engine, turbo-prop Merlin Fairchild 300 plane was making a normal approach to Tri-City Regional Airport, when it disappeared from the airport's radar screen.

Within minutes, word began circulating among the Winston Cup family that the Hooters plane was down and Alan was feared aboard. Shock waves rippled through the tight-knit group of people that comprise the competitors, teams, sponsors and media who live together on the road during the season.

Finally, confirmation came that indeed, the sport had lost its reigning champion.

Few slept that evening. And for those who did, it was fitful, at best.

At the track the next day, all knew the

Bobby Hillin's Heilig-Meyers Ford wears some of the scars every car receives at Bristol.

race would—and must—go on. Crew members stood *en masse* on pit road that morning, watching the Hooters transporter complete a memorial lap in honor of Alan and his three friends who were on the plane with him.

There was practice to be held and qualifying to be completed, but no one's heart was in it. Media members knew they had interviews to do to com-

plete stories about Alan and his team, but there was no joy in the assignment. Most had become friends with Alan in the years he struggled to become successful. All had enjoyed his humor and his candor. Like the other drivers and crew members, they had lost more than just an acquaintance. They had lost a champion and a friend.

To match the mood in the garage and the grandstands, the weather was ugly. Gray, gloomy clouds hung over the track spitting snow early in the day. When Harry Gant moved off pit road as the first qualifier, the temperature was 34 degrees.

Qualifying finally ended, and Rusty Wallace had won the pole—although he admitted it was the first time he had been the fastest qualifier and was not happy about it. "How could anybody be excited about today after what happened last night?" he rhetorically asked bystanders.

Brett Bodine would start alongside Wallace,

And when the green flag finally flew for the Food City 500, Rusty wasted no time in proving that, this day, he would be difficult to beat.

Even a tussle with Brett Bodine, which ended with Bodine spinning, would not deter Wallace from victory.

With his Miller Pontiac at the point, he gobbled the laps in huge chunks, finally leading six times for 376 of the 500 laps. He had to be good. Earnhardt and Mark Martin would have his lunch if he faltered at all.

Martin's hopes ended with a flat tire 60 laps from the end. Earnhardt's hopes of a second-straight win came down to the final 16 laps after the 17th caution, but Wallace was able to pull away to a .82-second victory. It was Earnhardt's third second place of the young season.

Behind Earnhardt came Kyle Petty, Jimmy Spencer, Davey Allison and Darrell Waltrip, all on the lead lap, while Morgan Shepherd was seventh, a single lap in ar-

Lake Speed gets crossed up at Bristol. His Purex Ford finished 29th.

with Ernie Irvan third-fastest in his team's backyard. Morgan Shepherd, Geoff Bodine and NASCAR Winston Cup point-leader Earnhardt were fourth, fifth and sixth.

After Michael Waltrip won Saturday's Busch Grand National race in his Pennzoil Pontiac, he made a lap in the opposite direction in memory of Kulwicki—and in victory lane, through his tears, the long-time bachelor asked friend Elizabeth "Buffy" Franks to marry him. She accepted. Waltrip's lap became the way Kulwicki's peers would honor and remember him throughout the remainder of the year.

With his finishes in the first five races of the year, Earnhardt had served notice to his fellow competitors that he would be difficult to beat in this year's battle for racing's most prestigious title.

At Bristol, Rusty Wallace proved he was ready to accept Earnhardt's challenge.

rears. Martin finished eighth, while Brett Bodine and Rick Mast completed the top ten.

When it was over, Wallace wheeled his black Pontiac around on the start/finish line, blinked back his tears, and began his "Polish Victory Lap" in honor of Kulwicki.

"To win this race was a big deal, but it is even a bigger deal to win it for my buddy Alan," Wal-

lace explained after the event. "We came from the midwest together, where we ran against each other for years.

"We both came to NASCAR Winston Cup, we both won Rookie of the Year and we both realized our dreams to be NASCAR Winston Cup Champions. He was my buddy.

"I dedicate this race to him and his family, along with the others who were on the plane with him. I don't want my good run to overshadow what happened to him.

"He was a good guy and did things his way. He concentrated on what he wanted and he got it. It's just a shame that what he did last year has been taken away from him and us so quickly."

Wallace turned from the interview and found friend and Miller public relations representative Tom Roberts on the victory podium. The two tried to smile at each other, but it was faltering. Roberts' company also worked with Kulwicki and Hooters and Tom had been Alan's mentor when he first came to NASCAR Winston Cup with Quincy's sponsorship, one car and two motors in his rookie season. Roberts had been scheduled to be on Kulwicki's plane, but at the last minute, had changed his plans and flown commercial to Bristol.

Roberts and Wallace stood behind the winner's trophy, arms around each other's shoulders, and tried to smile through their tears for the cameras.

It was nearly impossible. Alan was in their thoughts. They had lost their buddy.

The sport had lost its Champion.

Brett Bodine and Rusty Wallace brought the field to the green flag on the concrete Bristol surface.

The entire throng stood in silent prayer before the start of the race in remembrance of the sport's defending champion, Alan Kulwicki.

An early-race tangle sent Harry Gant and Joe Ruttman spinning on Bristol's high banks.

Fin. Pos.	Str. Pos.	Driver	Team	Fin. Pos.	Str. Pos.	Driver	Team
1	1	Rusty Wallace	Miller Genuine Draft Pontiac	19	27	Joe Ruttman	Fina Lube Ford
2	6	Dale Earnhardt	GM Goodwrench Chevrolet	20	17	Sterling Marlin	Raybestos Brakes Ford
3	14	Kyle Petty	Mello Yello Pontiac	21	18	Terry Labonte	Kellogg's Chevrolet
4	28	Jimmy Spencer	Meineke Mufflers Ford	22	34	Dick Trickle	Carolina Pottery Ford
5	10	Davey Allison	Havoline Ford	23	3	Ernie Irvan	Kodak Film Chevrolet
6	35	Darrell Waltrip	Western Auto Chevrolet	24	33	Bobby Labonte	Maxwell House Ford
7	4	Morgan Shepherd	Citgo Ford	25	24	Rick Wilson	STP Pontiac
8	8	Mark Martin	Valvoline Ford	26	9	Ricky Rudd	Tide Chevrolet
9	2	Brett Bodine	Quaker State Ford	27	23	Hut Stricklin	McDonald's Ford
10	19	Rick Mast	Skoal Classic Ford	28	26	Harry Gant	Skoal Bandit Chevrolet
11	25	Wally Dallenbach	Keystone Beer Ford	29	16	Lake Speed	Purex Ford
12	12	Derrike Cope	Bojangles' Ford	30	20	Bill Elliott	Budweiser Ford
13	30	Kenny Wallace	Dirt Devil Pontiac	31	29	Phil Parsons	Manheim Auctions Chevrolet
14	15	Michael Waltrip	Pennzoil Pontiac	32	22	Dale Jarrett	Interstate Batteries Chevrolet
15	32	Ted Musgrave	Jasper Engines Ford	33	13	Bobby Hillin	Heilig-Meyers Ford
16	31	Jimmy Means	NAPA Ford	34	7	Ken Schrader	Kodiak Chevrolet
17	21	Jeff Gordon	DuPont Auto Finishes Chevrolet	35	11	Bobby Hamilton	Country Time Ford
18	5	Geoff Bodine	Motorcraft Ford				

FIRST UNION 400

Rusty Wallace had plenty of time to savor his Bristol victory and the "Polish Victory Lap" he dedicated to his friend and fellow competitor, Alan Kulwicki. The NASCAR Winston Cup teams had a weekend off between Bristol and the next stop on the tour, the First Union 400 at North Wilkesboro Speedway.

As the rigs unloaded, there was a familiar sight in the garage area—the orange and white transporter of Alan Kulwicki Racing.

But the paint on the outside of the 18-wheeler didn't tell the real story of what had transpired during the two weeks following the death of the defending NASCAR Winston Cup Champion.

In Alan's typical, organized style, he had put his business and personal affairs in order. Fellow car-owner and close friend Felix Sabates had been appointed administrator of Alan's estate, and he left ownership of his race team to his father, former USAC championship engine builder Gerald.

Following Alan's funeral in Milwaukee, Sabates announced that the

Pole-sitter Brett Bodine established himself early in the event at Enoch Staley's North Wilkesboro Speedway.

Dale Earnhardt shares a stolen minute with wife Teresa.

team would be sold—and that Jimmy Hensley would drive the Kulwicki Racing Ford, at the express wishes of Alan, who had told team members and Sabates that if anything happened to him, he would like to see Hensley in the car.

At the same time, a combination of factors, including the loss of three key corporate personnel (including Hooters' chairman Robert Brooks' son, Mark) prompted Hooters to withdraw from the race team, leaving the door open to return to the sport in the future.

At North Wilkesboro, the Ford was rolled out

early '70s, brothers Brett and Geoff Bodine shared the front row for the start of the 400-lapper at Enoch Staley's .625 mile track.

Right behind the Bodines were Ernie Irvan and Kenny Schrader, making it Ford-Ford-Chevy-Chevy in the first four positions. Hut Stricklin, responding to the heat of driving for Junior Johnson in his backyard, put his McDonald's Ford in fifth place on the grid, inside Terry Labonte's Kellogg's Chevrolet. Rookie Jeff Gordon qualified seventh, with Sterling Marlin eighth, Rusty Wallace ninth and Ricky Rudd tenth.

Kyle Petty avoids the mess as rookie Jeff Gordon's day at North Wilkesboro comes to an early end.

of the AKR transporter bearing the familiar number 7, with "Easter Seals" emblazoned on the hood and "Bojangles'" on the rear quarter panels. Hensley would drive the Ford for the foreseeable future—at least until the team was sold.

When qualifying was completed, Hensley had put the Ford in 13th place, comfortably ahead of hotshots like Bill Elliott, Jimmy Spencer, Harry Gant, Kyle Petty, Darrell Waltrip, Davey Allison—and Dale Earnhardt!

For the first time since Bobby and Donnie Allison shared the front row at Rockingham in the

Geoff Bodine couldn't wait for the race to start. He had won the October race here last year in runaway fashion, pulling away to lead all but 13 of the final 275 laps in a race that remarkably ran caution-free on Monday after being rained out Sunday afternoon.

Bodine may have been in the familiar red Motorcraft Ford—but that's where the similarities ended this time!

On the first lap, entering the third turn, Geoff collided with Irvan. The red Ford, facing on-coming traffic, had a great view of the chaos taking place with the rest of the pack.

Irvan suffered brake damage after Schrader collected the Kodak Chevrolet and Mark Martin's crew took more than 50 laps to get him back on the track. Dick Trickle's day in the RahMoc Ford came to a quick end as well.

For the first half of the race, Sterling Marlin looked like he was headed for his first NASCAR Winston Cup victory after more than 250 starts—but his Raybestos Ford faded from the hunt in the last 150

Brothers Geoff and Brett Bodine shared the front row for the start of the First Union 400.

Dale Earnhardt looks for a way past Phil Parsons and Jimmy Spencer in the First Union 400.

laps after he had led the most laps of any driver that day—190!

As Marlin faded, Rusty Wallace, with unusual patience, brought his Miller Pontiac to the front—and once there, his pit crew kept him there—particularly during the final 100 laps of the race.

The final yellow flag flew with just 20 laps to

go—with Wallace leading by nearly six seconds over a battling Kyle Petty. Wallace didn't want to see that yellow, because his Pontiac took at least 15 laps for its tires to "come in." And he knew that the other eight drivers on the lead lap would all have an excellent shot at passing him for victory.

When the green came out for the 15-lap sprint, Petty, Schrader, Davey Allison and Darrell Waltrip lined up behind Wallace—and Rusty got the jump at the start, leaving the others to battle for the scraps.

Schrader pressed Kyle for second place—and as the battle ensued, Wallace pulled away to a 1.5-second victory, and another chance to complete the backwards victory lap in honor of Kulwicki.

Petty won the battle for second, with Davey Allison right behind Schrader and just ahead of Darrell. Terry Labonte came home sixth, ahead of Rudd and Morgan Shepherd, with Marlin the final driver on the lead lap.

Hensley, slightly involved in the first-lap melee, brought the AKR Ford home 12th in his first race behind the wheel.

The victory was the third for Wallace in the

box after the race, said he felt his team could win as many as ten races before the season was over. He reiterated his feelings that his team was of championship caliber and if he could avoid finishes like the one at Daytona in February, he expected to contend for the title.

Allison's third fourth place in the race was his third top-five finish of the season, and he moved from fifth to third in the standings, while Kyle Petty used his second place to climb from eighth to

Bill Elliott was a favorite in Junior Johnson's backyard, but he could only manage a 10th-place finish.

young season. Dale Earnhardt fought his Goodwrench Chevrolet all day, but finally came home to a four-lap-in-arrears, 16th-place position. With his victory, Rusty moved to the front of the NASCAR Winston Cup point table.

The Pontiac driver was 18 points ahead after the first seven races of the season, and in the press

fourth in the points. The first-lap wreck dropped Geoff Bodine from third to sixth in the points while Mark Martin fell from fourth to seventh.

The next stop on the tour was Martinsville—and after two consecutive short-track victories, Wallace couldn't wait to get to Virginia for the final race of the first swing through the bullrings.

Rusty shares victory lane with Jim Roper, winner of the very first NASCAR Winston Cup race at the old Charlotte Fairgrounds in 1948.

Fin. Pos.	Str. Pos.	Driver	Team	Fin. Pos.	Str. Pos.	Driver	Team
1	9	Rusty Wallace	Miller Genuine Draft Pontiac	18	28	Phil Parsons	Manheim Auctions Chevrolet
2	22	Kyle Petty	Mello Yello Pontiac	19	25	Rick Mast	Skoal Classic Ford
3	4	Ken Schrader	Kodiak Chevrolet	20	20	Michael Waltrip	Pennzoil Pontiac
4	27	Davey Allison	Havoline Ford	21	33	Wally Dallenbach	Keystone Beer Ford
5	23	Darrell Waltrip	Western Auto Chevrolet	22	5	Hut Stricklin	McDonald's Ford
6	6	Terry Labonte	Kellogg's Chevrolet	23	26	Rick Wilson	STP Pontiac
7	10	Ricky Rudd	Tide Chevrolet	24	31	Ted Musgrave	Jasper Engines Ford
8	17	Morgan Shepherd	Citgo Ford	25	30	Bobby Labonte	Maxwell House Ford
9	8	Sterling Marlin	Raybestos Brakes Ford	26	32	Bobby Hillin	Heilig-Meyers Ford
10	15	Bill Elliott	Budweiser Ford	27	34	Jimmy Means	NAPA Ford
11	3	Ernie Irvan	Kodak Film Chevrolet	28	2	Geoff Bodine	Motorcraft Ford
12	13	Jimmy Hensley	Bojangles' Ford	29	29	Bobby Hamilton	Country Time Ford
13	19	Harry Gant	Skoal Bandit Chevrolet	30	18	Derrike Cope	Bojangles' Ford
14	14	Jimmy Spencer	Meineke Mufflers Ford	31	12	Mark Martin	Valvoline Ford
15	24	Kenny Wallace	Dirt Devil Pontiac	32	11	Dale Jarrett	Interstate Batteries Chevrolet
16	21	Dale Earnhardt	GM Goodwrench Chevrolet	33	16	Dick Trickle	Carolina Pottery Ford
17	1	Brett Bodine	Quaker State Ford	34	7	Jeff Gordon	DuPont Auto Finishes Chevrolet

Hut Stricklin's sparkling front-row qualifying position came to naught with a 26th-place finish. Pole-sitter Geoff Bodine would finish sixth.

For four days, the team from Spartanburg, SC, did yeoman work, rebuilding the red Motorcraft Ford Geoff Bodine had stuffed into the third-turn wall at North Wilkesboro. The car needed a new rear clip, among other items, and when the crew completed its work, Geoff slid through the window for qualifying at Clay Earles' impeccable Martinsville Speedway.

Bodine blistered the track record early in the session, and then headed off to join brother Brett atop a van inside turn four to watch the remainder of the field try to unseat him from his first pole position since Phoenix 1991.

And after everyone had failed, Brett turned to Geoff, shook his hand and welcomed him back to the Busch Clash. A regular in the

Part of the field gets by as Bobby Hamilton
spins in Martinsville's fourth turn.

February dash for cash since the first year he was eligible in 1982, Bodine had missed this past February's running of the event because he had failed to win a pole in 1992.

When qualifying was over, Bodine's new track record of 99.887 miles per hour gave additional pleasure to his car owner. It was the first time a Bud Moore Ford had been on a pole—anywhere—since Ricky Rudd did it in 1986! Bud headed for the DuPont golf course with a huge grin.

The closest thing to Bodine was another red Ford—with Golden Arches on it. Hut Stricklin would start from the front row for the first time in his NASCAR Winston Cup career, just ahead of rookie Jeff Gordon, continuing his outstanding qualifying in the young season.

Kyle Petty continued to ride his hot streak, putting the Mello Yello Pontiac fourth on the grid, just ahead of Rusty Wallace and Davey Allison in

a battle of the black cars.

Jimmy Hensley, the local hero, lived up to his billing in the AKR Ford, putting the Bojangles'-sponsored Thunderbird seventh-fastest in the field. Mark Martin would start the race eighth, Bobby Hamilton was a surprising ninth and Michael Waltrip's Pennzoil Pontiac rounded out the ten fastest cars.

With the public address blaring "Kansas City, Here I Come!" and grand marshal Joe Montana riding in the back of a Pontiac convertible with Miss Winston, Brooke Sealey, the field rumbled to life.

Despite the promise shown by the two red Fords, the real question was whether anyone had an answer to Rusty Wallace on the short tracks this season. Davey Allison had just nipped Rusty for the Richmond victory, but since then Wallace had nailed down back-to-back wins at Bristol and North Wilkesboro. His qualifying time made him a favorite for another victory this Sunday.

With Gerald and Thelma Kulwicki attending their first race since Alan's death, the question of whether Wallace could make it "All for April" quickly became evident.

Bodine's lead lasted just over a lap, when he spun in the second turn of the second lap. Stricklin went to the point, with Wallace right behind him—and it was at this point of the race, with Wallace pressing every foot of the half-mile track, that co-car owner Roger Penske gave the Pontiac driver some sage words of advice over the radio.

"He told me to cool it, that when the first pit stop came along our crew could get me out ahead of Hut—so that's what I did," Wallace explained. "And sure enough, when the time came, those guys on pit road gave me a great stop and put me out in the lead.

"From that point, all I wanted to do was make sure that I was patient and that I didn't over-extend the car. I was able to run hard through traffic—and when the car got hot and slippery, I could 'cool it' and make everything on the car—brakes, tires and all—work the way it was supposed to."

How dominant was Wallace in the 500-lap affair?

After he went to the front on lap 88, the only other lap leaders were Stricklin (once for one lap,) Dale Earnhardt (once for one lap) and Davey Allison (twice for two laps.) That was all. Wallace simply hammered the field into submission. His crew did its work as well, getting the Miller Pontiac on and off pit road at the front of the field.

Despite Wallace's complete domination of the race, the last ten laps gave him reason to worry about a third-straight victory.

Rusty watched a three-second lead evaporate with 14 laps to go when Brett Bodine spun and brought out the yellow. With just nine laps to go, the green flag waved and Rusty answered the call, punching the throttle and pulling away by five car lengths.

Then, with just three laps left and in command of the race, the yellow fell on the black Pontiac again. Morgan Shepherd had smacked the fourth turn wall and it looked like the race would end under the yellow flag.

Davey Allison gave it his best shot, pulling to within a fender as the two black cars raced to the yellow on lap 498. Rusty saw the Ford driver coming and held him off at the flagstand and as the cars circled around the final two times, it was the Miller Pontiac at the point.

Winston Cup racing always brings a packed house to Clay Earles' Martinsville.

son's Budweiser Ford, finished 27th after damage incurred in several incidents. His "teammate," Stricklin, watched his dreams of a top finish end with a broken rear end. Ernie Irvan cooked a head gasket. Jimmy Spencer and Harry Gant had engine problems end their days.

On the other hand, Jimmy Hensley brought the AKR Ford home 13th.

When all the point shuffling was over, Wallace was solidly in the lead after the first eight events. Davey Allison used his second place to move to within striking distance of Dale Earnhardt for second in the standings. Kyle Petty was nine points ahead of Geoff Bodine for fourth place in the points.

The first round of the short tracks was over. Wallace had won three consecutive races. Now the fun was about to begin. Talladega, Sears Point and Charlotte loomed large on the horizon.

Could Wallace make it four-straight wins and build on his point lead?

The battle for the win. With the race ending under caution, Rusty Wallace barely beat Davey Allison to the stripe.

Behind Allison came Dale Jarrett and Darrell Waltrip, the only other cars on the lead lap, while Kyle Petty, who had lost a lap on a green flag stop when the yellow came out two laps later, was fifth.

Geoff Bodine's high hopes for a win were gone early in the race, but he gamely brought the Motorcraft Ford home in sixth place after a late-race battle with brother Brett. Jeff Gordon and Terry Labonte had their own private war, with Gordon winning the eighth-place struggle. Mark Martin completed the top ten.

Where were the big guns? Dale Earnhardt, running second to Wallace, had engine problems strike his black Chevrolet on lap 318. He was classified 22nd, and fell 106 points behind Wallace in the championship battle.

Bill Elliott, off to a slow start with Junior John-

Activity is furious in very close quarters on Martinsville's pit road.

The Miller crew's celebration began on pit road after Rusty's victory.

Fin. Pos.	Str. Pos.	Driver	Team	Fin. Pos.	Str. Pos.	Driver	Team
1	5	Rusty Wallace	Miller Genuine Draft Pontiac	18	13	Ken Schrader	Kodiak Chevrolet
2	6	Davey Allison	Havoline Ford	19	29	Morgan Shepherd	Citgo Ford
3	11	Dale Jarrett	Interstate Batteries Chevrolet	20	28	Phil Parsons	Manheim Auctions Chevrolet
4	26	Darrell Waltrip	Western Auto Chevrolet	21	30	Sterling Marlin	Raybestos Brakes Ford
5	4	Kyle Petty	Mello Yello Pontiac	22	21	Dale Earnhardt	GM Goodwrench Chevrolet
6	1	Geoff Bodine	Motorcraft Ford	23	31	Bobby Hillin	Heilig-Meyers Ford
7	18	Brett Bodine	Quaker State Ford	24	15	Kenny Wallace	Dirt Devil Pontiac
8	3	Jeff Gordon	DuPont Auto Finishes Chevrolet	25	27	Derrike Cope	Bojangles' Ford
9	19	Terry Labonte	Kellogg's Chevrolet	26	2	Hut Stricklin	McDonald's Ford
10	8	Mark Martin	Valvoline Ford	27	16	Bill Elliott	Budweiser Ford
11	17	Rick Mast	Skoal Classic Ford	28	22	Ted Musgrave	Jasper Engines Ford
12	24	Bobby Labonte	Maxwell House Ford	29	14	Ricky Rudd	Tide Chevrolet
13	7	Jimmy Hensley	Bojangles' Ford	30	25	Jimmy Spencer	Meineke Mufflers Ford
14	32	Dick Trickle	Carolina Pottery Ford	31	23	Harry Gant	Skoal Bandit Chevrolet
15	34	Dave Marcis	Swanson Chevrolet	32	12	Ernie Irvan	Kodak Film Chevrolet
16	10	Michael Waltrip	Pennzoil Pontiac	33	9	Bobby Hamilton	Country Time Ford
17	20	Rick Wilson	STP Pontiac	34	33	Wally Dallenbach	Keystone Beer Ford

WINSTON 500

**TALLADEGA
SUPERSPEEDWAY**

MAY 2, 1993

*F*aced with a 106-point deficit and poor finishes the previous two races, everyone expected Dale Earnhardt to arrive at Talladega for the Winston 500 loaded for bear. One only had to remember a few short weeks ago to recall what Earnhardt had done at Daytona with his superspeedway program. There was no reason to feel the "Big E" would be any less dominant at the 2.66-mile track.

Even so, no one expected Dale to win the pole. Qualifying has never been one of Earnhardt's strongest suits and although he is more often at the front of the field than at the rear, his record of 13 poles in more than 425 career starts speaks for itself.

The Winston 500 always means two things to teams. It is a return to the fastest track on the circuit after a month spent on the bullrings.

And it is the second round of the Winston Million, R.J. Reynolds' $1 million bonus posted each year to the driver able to win three of four specific races in that season.

A second lost on pit road can translate into the length of a football field on the track at Talladega.

Earnhardt jumps away from the huge pack of traffic in the early laps of the Winston 500.

Dale Jarrett was not able to capitalize on the second leg of the Winston Million event.

Dale Jarrett had become the first qualifier for the award with his victory at the Daytona 500 by STP. If he could win here and then triumph in either the Coca-Cola 600 at Charlotte or the Mountain Dew Southern 500 at Darlington, he would join Bill Elliott as the second winner of the Winston Million.

If no driver is able to win the Million, the first driver to win two of the four events receives a $100,000 "consolation" bonus from Winston. So if Jarrett could win at Talladega, he would "lock" that $100,000 regardless of whether he won either of the remaining races.

Still, the hottest driver in the garage area was Rusty Wallace—who was quick to point out that prior to his Daytona tumbling act, he had come from the back of the pack to a challenging top-five position. There was no doubt in his mind that he had a car capable of amassing four consecutive NASCAR Winston Cup victories.

After the first qualifying session (interrupted twice by rain) was completed, the message had been given. Earnhardt was back—and had blistered the competition to win his first pole since Watkins Glen the previous August. (He had started from the point at Darlington, but that position was based on points after qualifying was rained out.)

The Goodwrench Chevrolet was not merely at the front of the field. Earnhardt had clobbered the competition. He was a mile an hour faster than second-fastest Jimmy Spencer—and that mile per hour translated to nearly a half-second, a bulge unheard of at the faster tracks on the tour.

How much is that half-second? From Spencer to 20th-place Bobby Labonte, the gap was just .0368 seconds!

Earnhardt had hung the "Driver to Beat" sign around his neck for the remainder of the weekend.

Behind Spencer came Jarrett, looking for a boost toward the million-dollar bonus. Rick Wilson was fourth-quickest, showing once again that Petty Enterprises hadn't forgotten how to build a fast superspeedway car. Davey Allison was fifth-fastest at his home track, with a surprising Joe Ruttman sixth-fastest in Dick Moroso's Ford.

Where were Wallace and others like Kyle Petty? Back in the second half of the field for Sunday's 188-lapper. Petty's Mello Yello Pontiac engine turned up with a fever when it came time for qualifying.

One new face in the line-up for the Winston 500 was Greg Sacks, taking over the Country Time Lemonade Ford from Bobby Hamilton, who

four-wide, thrilling the fans—and making every driver in the field earn his money that day as he put his utmost trust and faith in those all around him. It was unbelievable.

Finally, Earnhardt, Spencer, Wilson and Ruttman broke free, and in single file, drew away from the pack far enough to make the rest of the field see that three-wide would merely let the leaders get away. The rest shuffled their way into a single file, and then began to catch the leaders.

Still, those first five laps were the stuff of

Davey Allison hoped for victory in front of his home-state fans, but was forced to settle for seventh.

was released from his ride prior to the opening of qualifying.

Talladega is famous for the freight-train lines of drafting cars, but no one expected what was awaiting the huge throng of fans when the green flag fell for the first time Sunday.

Mark Martin had an electrical problem that kept his Valvoline Ford from firing on the line, and while the field was making its warm-up laps, Martin's crew straight-wired the problem switch. Mark went to the shotgun position in the field to start the race.

And what a start it was!

For the first four laps, the field ran three- and

which legends were made. Everyone emerged in great shape once sense began to prevail. The collective sigh of relief from car owners, drivers, crew members and fans was audible!

In typical Talladega fashion, the race quickly became a shuffling of leaders as drafting—and finding the right partner to run with—became the byword of the day.

Wallace, Martin and Ernie Irvan clawed their way toward the front, and all made it to the point as part of the 22 lead changes among seven drivers. Still, Earnhardt proved to be the stoutest of the group, moving back to the point eight times to lead the most laps and grab the five bonus points.

Irvan surfaced at the lead near halfway, leading the 91st lap before giving way to Earnhardt. Ernie went back to the front during a yellow flag on lap 134 and then hung with the leaders, hoping to find a way to win his second-straight event at Talladega. He had triumphed in the DieHard 500 in 1992 and wanted a second victory at the fastest super-speedway.

Giving chase to Earnhardt in the waning stages of the enormous tussle were Wallace, Jarrett and Mark Martin, who proved his car was capable after he found his way back to the front.

Spencer, having a solid run, began battling with Irvan as the two tried to sort out fourth place with just 14 laps to go. And as the pair struggled, the front three of Earnhardt, Wallace and Martin moved away, beginning to stretch their lead and preparing to sort out the victory among the Chevrolet, Pontiac and Ford.

Mother Nature, however, had other things in mind. With just eight laps remaining in the race, a rain shower on the backstretch brought out the final yellow flag of the day and Earnhardt busted past Wallace in the run to the caution flag—just in case the race was not restarted. After five laps, the cars were red-flagged to enable the race to finish under green.

After an 11-minute delay, the green flag fell for a two-lap shoot-out, and the fireworks began. Earnhardt was at the point, with Wallace second. Martin was third, followed by Irvan, and the latter two drafted up behind Wallace, with Martin trying to get past on the outside as they took the white flag for the final lap.

Rusty moved to block Martin and Irvan went low, getting a boost from Jimmy Spencer. That put the Kodak Chevrolet behind the Goodwrench Lumina and as Irvan tried to get past Earnhardt, the pair bumped in the first turn. Irvan slid through the hole, pulling Spencer with him, and the two battled to the finish, with Irvan ahead by two car-lengths for his first victory of the season.

Behind Irvan and Spencer the struggle ensued. Jarrett, Earnhardt and Wallace were in a huge battle, and as Dale moved down on the track in the trioval to protect his spot from Wallace, the two collided. Instantly, Wallace was repeating his Daytona tumbling act at the apron of the track. He was credited with a sixth-place finish.

Jarrett took third, losing his chance to clinch at least the $100,000 bonus from RJR. Earnhardt was fourth, while Ruttman turned in an impressive run to come home fifth and Davey Allison claimed seventh place. Completing the top-10 were Derrike Cope, Jimmy Hensley and Michael Waltrip, posting his first top-10 finish of the season in his Pennzoil Pontiac.

The win was the first for Irvan since his triumph here last August, and put him tenth in the point standings after nine races.

Despite his sixth-place finish, Wallace maintained his point lead, seeing it cut 20 points by Earnhardt to 86. Allison was third in the standings,

Darrell Waltrip looks for some handling tips from fellow Chevrolet driver Dale Earnhardt.

Ernie Irvan is all smiles after his shoot-out victory over Jimmy Spencer and Dale Jarrett at Talladega.

with Jarrett moving back into fourth place ahead of Kyle Petty, who finished 18th in the Winston 500.

Wallace's Pontiac wasn't the only car damaged at Talladega. Also involved in multi-car wrecks were Sterling Marlin, Geoff Bodine, Terry Labonte, Rick Mast, Greg Sacks, Hut Stricklin and Brett Bodine.

The battle at Talladega was over—as was Wallace's three-race winning streak. The road course in the California wine country was next on the schedule, and drivers and crew members headed back to their shops to load the left-right cars in preparation for the trans-continental run to the Bay Area.

Fin. Pos.	Str. Pos.	Driver	Team	Fin. Pos.	Str. Pos.	Driver	Team
1	16	Ernie Irvan	Kodak Film Chevrolet	22	10	Bill Elliott	Budweiser Ford
2	2	Jimmy Spencer	Meineke Mufflers Ford	23	37	Harry Gant	Skoal Bandit Chevrolet
3	3	Dale Jarrett	Interstate Batteries Chevrolet	24	14	Sterling Marlin	Raybestos Brakes Ford
4	1	Dale Earnhardt	GM Goodwrench Chevrolet	25	34	Ritchie Petty	Winston Cup Water Ford
5	6	Joe Ruttman	Fina Lube Ford	26	33	Darrell Waltrip	Western Auto Chevrolet
6	24	Rusty Wallace	Miller Genuine Draft Pontiac	27	31	Geoff Bodine	Motorcraft Ford
7	5	Davey Allison	Havoline Ford	28	23	Ted Musgrave	Jasper Engines Ford
8	15	Derrike Cope	Bojangles' Ford	29	7	Wally Dallenbach	Keystone Beer Ford
9	29	Jimmy Hensley	Bojangles' Ford	30	12	Brett Bodine	Quaker State Ford
10	13	Michael Waltrip	Pennzoil Pontiac	31	27	Dick Trickle	Carolina Pottery Ford
11	30	Jeff Gordon	DuPont Auto Finishes Chevrolet	32	28	Jimmy Means	Hurley Limo Ford
12	11	Mark Martin	Valvoline Ford	33	22	Greg Sacks	Country Time Ford
13	19	Rick Mast	Skoal Classic Ford	34	32	Lake Speed	Purex Ford
14	17	Kenny Wallace	Dirt Devil Pontiac	35	20	Bobby Labonte	Maxwell House Ford
15	9	Morgan Shepherd	Citgo Ford	36	35	Jimmy Horton	Active Trucking Chevrolet
16	4	Rick Wilson	STP Pontiac	37	38	Terry Labonte	Kellogg's Chevrolet
17	41	Bobby Hillin	Heilig-Meyers Ford	38	36	Rich Bickle	Kraft Ford
18	21	Kyle Petty	Mello Yello Pontiac	39	18	Jeff Purvis	Phoenix Construction Chevrolet
19	39	Phil Parsons	Manheim Auctions Chevrolet	40	40	Ken Bouchard	Safety Kleen Ford
20	25	Hut Stricklin	McDonald's Ford	41	26	Ricky Rudd	Tide Chevrolet
21	8	Ken Schrader	Kodiak Chevrolet				

SAVE MART 300

F or the first four years, the NASCAR Winston Cup tour stop at Sears Point International Raceway came in mid-June, a perfect time for drivers and their families to enjoy the beauty of the California wine country and San Francisco. This year's event was scheduled a month earlier, however, adjusting the schedule for the inaugural NASCAR Winston Cup race at New Hampshire in July.

The four weeks made no difference with regard to the weather in the Bay Area. It was just as gorgeous as ever, and few could overcome the urge to spend a few hours wandering through one of the

Sears Point's track winds through scenic hillsides, offering great vantage points for fans.

Just days after purchasing Alan Kulwicki Racing,

Geoff Bodine celebrated his victory for

Bud Moore at Sears Point.

Dale Earnhardt proved the pundits wrong by winning the pole at Sears Point's road course. Ricky Rudd started from the second-fastest qualifying position.

world's most beautiful cities. From Chinatown to Fisherman's Wharf, from Pier 39 to Russian Hill, familiar faces were seen going the other way as the cable cars passed going up and down the fabled hills.

For those who had their fill of the city, there were trips to the Napa and Sonoma Valleys to enjoy; cruising from one winery to another in some of the most beautiful countryside America has to offer.

Never lost in those few hours stolen from the hectic NASCAR Winston Cup schedule, however, were thoughts of the upcoming test on the serpentine road course.

Over the past two decades, drivers had taken turns showing their prowess on road courses. Richard Petty, Bobby Allison, Darrell Waltrip were the Riverside masters. Terry Labonte and Rusty Wallace, along with Ricky Rudd, began strutting their stuff in the Southern California desert, before land owners turned the track into a housing development.

At Sears Point, Rudd and Wallace notched the first two victories, with Davey Allison scoring his only road course victory the third year after the controversial finish with Rudd.

Last June, Ernie Irvan had made a triumphant return to his home state, coming from worst to first in a scintillating victory after a stop-and-go penalty for jumping the start of the race.

Sears Point has always had its drama. This year would be no different.

After going, in his own words, "butt-over-teacup" at Talladega, NASCAR Winston Cup point-leader Wallace had a six-inch pin in his left wrist and would drive with a special brace to provide support for the injury. SCCA Trans-Am series champion Scott Sharp would stand by to relieve Wallace if he needed help in the 74-lap race.

In the week prior to the Save Mart 300, it was announced that Geoff Bodine was the buyer for Kulwicki Racing, and Geoff said that he would continue the season in Bud Moore's Motorcraft Ford while the Kulwicki Racing effort would continue with Jimmy Hensley in the car, except for road courses in which Tommy Kendall would clamber through the window.

Wally Dallenbach had been wearing a grin for a month. He knew his best chance for a victory on the tour would be at either Sears Point or Watkins

Glen because of his road racing background. And he knew that Jack Roush's Fords had proven to be awesome machines at road course venues. Roush had won numerous road racing titles, and Wally could barely contain his excitement.

As practice opened, the "favorites" pool included Rudd, Wallace, Labonte, Irvan, Martin, Darrell, Kendall and Dallenbach. Few gave a thought to a black Chevrolet.

Everyone overlooks Earnhardt when it comes to road races. They shouldn't. Dale may not be as flashy as some when it comes to turning left and right, but he does a more than adequate job. And when it came to qualifying in the Sonoma Valley, he put it all together to smash Ricky Rudd's track record by nearly a mile per hour and notch his sec-

With his team making furious preparations on his back-up car, Brett Bodine was unable to make a first-round qualifying run. He bent his primary Quaker State Ford in a practice wreck. And Kendall, who many felt would have an excellent shot at the pole, did just that for most of his lap. But he went into the tire barrier in the 11th turn—trashing the nose of his Ford—and Paul Andrews and crew pulled the back-up Kulwicki Racing Ford off the transporter.

With the enormous crowd of more than 90,000 still finding its way to viewing spots on the hill-

The hillsides were packed as the biggest crowd in Sears Point history turned out for the race.

ond-straight Busch Pole.

Rudd was right behind, while Geoff Bodine celebrated his purchase of Kulwicki Racing by qualifying inside the second row, alongside Irvan. Martin and Wallace made up the third row—an outstanding effort from Rusty—while Dallenbach's grin just got wider and wider after his seventh-quickest lap. Ken Schrader, Allison and Labonte completed the top-10 on the 2.52-mile track.

sides overlooking Sears Point, the field rolled away for the fifth time in the valley northeast of San Francisco.

Earnhardt immediately showed that his fast qualifying lap was not a fluke. He refused to yield the lead and commanded the race for the first 16 laps before Geoff Bodine squeezed past.

During green flag stops, Rusty Wallace, Michael Waltrip and Sterling Marlin held the lead briefly, until the cycle was complete. Earnhardt was once again in command and the Goodwrench driver seemed headed for the first road course victory in his illustrious career.

But when Tommy Kendall was knocked sideways at the top of the hill in the second turn, Earnhardt had nowhere to go—and hammered Kendall's Ford.

While Earnhardt was doing his best to recover, Geoff Bodine went past to the lead. He stretched the lead to a few car-lengths and seemed headed for his first victory of the season—until the final yellow flag flew just three laps from the end of the race when Dorsey Schroeder, in the Country Time Lemonade Ford, wrecked in the entrance to the seventh turn and had to be towed off the track.

That set up a one-lap dash, with the green and white flags being displayed simultaneously as the race restarted. There were but 2.52 miles to go, but Bodine knew he was in trouble. Rudd and Irvan were right behind him and the start was critical to the Ford driver.

Up the hill they went, with Rudd right on Bodine's bumper. Between the fourth and fifth turns, Rudd hammered Bodine in the rear bumper, sending the Ford into a frantic swerve. Bodine recovered, pulled back in front of the Tide Chevrolet and then watched Rudd and Irvan get into a sec-

ond-place battle in the Carousel. All Geoff needed to do then was not make a mistake.

The second half of the lap was uneventful and the red Ford came home .63 seconds ahead of the second-place battle, won by Irvan.

The victory was the first on a road course for a Bud Moore car since Rudd won the 1985 Winston Western 500 at Riverside!

Bodine confessed after the race that the win was extra-sweet for him, because he had bought Alan Kulwicki's team during the week before the race, and this was the first chance he had to drive a "backwards" victory lap in honor of Alan.

"It was special to me because I had watched Rusty Wallace do it three times and I wanted the chance to do it for Alan myself," an emotional Bodine said after the race. "The timing was perfect—it couldn't have been better. I was able to show my respect for Alan that way."

Behind Bodine, Irvan and Rudd came Schrader and Kyle. Earnhardt salvaged sixth place after the Kendall entanglement, while Dallenbach was seventh, Rick Wilson eighth, Terry Labonte ninth and Hut Stricklin tenth. A total of 14 cars were on the lead lap.

Sadly for Wallace, his hopes of maintaining the NASCAR Winston Cup point lead went up in

Ted Musgrave cranks his Ford through the turn at the top of the hill in northern California.

transmission smoke halfway through the race. His Miller Pontiac was classified 38th and he fell to second in the point battle. Earnhardt had capitalized on a 100-point swing to move back into a 20-point lead.

Despite a 15th-place finish, Davey Allison remained third in the standings while Petty's sixth-place finish moved him to fourth.

The holiday in the Bay Area was over. Cable car rides would have to wait until next year. Things were starting to get serious with a third of the season in the books—and a fortnight at Charlotte beckoned.

In the final laps of the race, Geoff Bodine left Ricky Rudd and Ernie Irvan to battle for second place. Irvan edged Rudd for the bridesmaid's position.

Fin. Pos.	Str. Pos.	Driver	Team	Fin. Pos.	Str. Pos.	Driver	Team
1	3	Geoff Bodine	Motorcraft Ford	23	16	Michael Waltrip	Pennzoil Pontiac
2	4	Ernie Irvan	Kodak Film Chevrolet	24	26	Brett Bodine	Quaker State Ford
3	2	Ricky Rudd	Tide Chevrolet	25	14	P.J. Jones	Melling Performance Ford
4	8	Ken Schrader	Kodiak Chevrolet	26	34	Bill Sedgwick	Spears Motorsports Chevrolet
5	18	Kyle Petty	Mello Yello Pontiac	27	22	Jimmy Spencer	Meineke Mufflers Ford
6	1	Dale Earnhardt	GM Goodwrench Chevrolet	28	25	Dave Marcis	Pronto Auto Parts Chevrolet
7	7	Wally Dallenbach	Keystone Beer Ford	29	31	Rick Mast	Skoal Classic Ford
8	20	Rick Wilson	STP Pontiac	30	39	Dirk Stephens	Pepsi/Mark's Drywall Ford
9	10	Terry Labonte	Kellogg's Chevrolet	31	28	Bill Schmitt	Nevada City Spring Water Ford
10	36	Hut Stricklin	McDonald's Ford	32	27	Butch Gilliland	Gear Engineering Chevrolet
11	15	Jeff Gordon	DuPont Auto Finishes Chevrolet	33	19	Dorsey Schroeder	Country Time Ford
12	23	Sterling Marlin	Raybestos Brakes Ford	34	29	John Krebs	Diamond Ridge Racing Chevrolet
13	32	Dale Jarrett	Interstate Batteries Chevrolet	35	13	Darrell Waltrip	Western Auto Chevrolet
14	12	Morgan Shepherd	Citgo Ford	36	21	Kenny Wallace	Dirt Devil Pontiac
15	9	Davey Allison	Havoline Ford	37	37	Phil Parsons	Manheim Auctions Chevrolet
16	41	Bobby Labonte	Maxwell House Ford	38	6	Rusty Wallace	Miller Genuine Draft Pontiac
17	17	Bill Elliott	Budweiser Ford	39	24	Ted Musgrave	Jasper Engines Ford
18	11	Derrike Cope	Bojangles' Ford	40	5	Mark Martin	Valvoline Ford
19	35	Harry Gant	Skoal Bandit Chevrolet	41	30	Bobby Hillin	Heilig-Meyers Ford
20	38	Dick Trickle	Carolina Pottery Ford	42	40	Jeff Davis	Van-K Karting Wheels Ford
21	43	Rick Carelli	Chesrown Auto Group Chevrolet	43	42	Hershel McGriff	J.T. Carriers, Inc. Chevrolet
22	33	Tommy Kendall	Family Channel Ford				

CHARLOTTE MOTOR SPEEDWAY

MAY 24, 1993

When The Winston was created by the folks at R.J. Reynolds as a special, non-points race to show appreciation to the stalwart fans of NASCAR Winston Cup racing, all hoped it would grow into a classic event that matched the best of the series in an affair that showcased their talents.

The first running of The Winston saw Darrell Waltrip cook the engine in his Junior Johnson Chevrolet at the start/finish line after running down Harry Gant in the final two laps.

Geoff Bodine, Bill Elliott and Dale Earnhardt tangled in the 1987 running, followed by Rusty Wallace and Darrell Waltrip duking it out in Charlotte's fourth turn in 1989.

It got even better than that when Davey Allison and Kyle Petty

A pair of outstanding pit stops during qualifying helped Ernie Irvan and Rusty Wallace to front-row starts for The Winston.

Rick Mast on his way to a fifth place finish in The Winston.

battled their way across the finish line in 1992, the first year the event was run under the Charlotte lights. Who will ever forget Allison winning in a shower of sparks?

The hype that surrounds the race grows each year, and each May, more than 100,000 fans show up at Charlotte to see what will happen in this unique event.

After the Petty/Allison fireworks in 1992, few thought The Winston would ever see a finish quite as spectacular.

But those who felt that way hadn't paid much attention to the record book. Every three years, the same guy won the event. And this was the third year. The guy in question is the very same one who, once the bit is put between his teeth, is perhaps the most difficult person to beat in the modern history of Winston Cup racing.

Sure, Richard Petty won 200. David Pearson was the fox. Bobby Allison was as crafty as they come. There were few more gutsy when clench-jaw time arrived than Cale Yarborough.

But Dale Earnhardt is one-of-a-kind. And he was proving this year that he might also just be one-for-the-ages.

The Winston, with its 70-lap length divided into segments of 30, 30 and 10 laps (the final all

green-flag) seems designed to bring out the best in Earnhardt.

And Earnhardt will be the first to tell you that The Winston is special. Because it awards no points, the race cannot affect a driver's standing—or the year-end point fund distribution. It is, however, a rich payday, with $200,000 going to the winner. And that kind of money still brings out the best in a driver.

"It's The Winston," Earnhardt explained as simply as he could. "You race the first two segments to get yourself in shape to have a chance to win the final segment. And then you race like hell over those last 10 laps."

That simplistic philosophy came to bear at Charlotte.

The night qualifying session is one of the other unique aspects of The Winston weekend. The entire team's performance is incorporated into determining the starting position for the car in the first segment.

The driver makes three laps, and must make a right-side, two-tire pit stop in the middle of the qualifying effort. Normally, drivers are limited to 55 miles per hour on pit road—but The Winston isn't "normal"—as Rusty Wallace was quick to show his peers.

After Earnhardt and his "Flying Aces" turned the quickest time (including a blistering 11.38-second stop for tires) it was time for Wallace to unveil his surprise.

He absolutely scorched pit road on both ends, and that, combined with a 10.84-second stop, put him on the pole. For a minute, that is.

The only problem was that Ernie Irvan was standing in Wallace's pit, watching the Miller Pontiac driver hustle off and on pit road. And it gave him an idea of what he had to do if he wanted to put the Kodak Chevrolet on the pole.

And that's just what he did, with crew chief Tony Glover reminding him on the radio to "get that thing in here, and don't waste any time doing it."

Glover and the rest of the Kodak mighty-mites did their thing in the pits, and barely had time to celebrate a 10.73-second stop with high-fives before Irvan was whistling out of the fourth turn on his way to the pole.

Irvan, Wallace and Earnhardt were the quick three, with Bill Elliott fourth, two-time defending The Winston champion Davey Allison fifth and Kyle Petty sixth for the start of the all-star event.

The first 15 places on the grid for The Winston were filled by those who had previously qualified for the event, and the top five finishers from the Winston Open would join the field, taking their places behind the others after the preliminary event.

The Open featured some excellent cars and drivers, with Jeff Gordon winning the pole by besting Brett Bodine, Rick Mast and Rick Wilson. Michael Waltrip was fifth-fastest, just ahead of Sterling Marlin and Phil Parsons, Derrike Cope and Jimmy Spencer. In all, 33 cars would try to grab one of the top five spots and advance into The Winston.

The Winston Open was scheduled for 50 laps, and when it was over, Sterling Marlin had become the first driver to win three Winston Opens, beating Kenny Schrader by a car length for the 16th starting slot in The Winston. Brett Bodine, Michael Waltrip and Rick Mast claimed the final spots for The Winston.

Sterling Marlin (8) looks for a way to victory lane in The Winston Open. By the time the race was over, he had found one.

When the green flag finally fell to start the first segment, Irvan blasted away from the pack, leading the first 30 laps and easily collecting the $50,000 bonus that went to the segment winner. So far, this was a great deal, Irvan thought after he took the first segment flag. "A total of 33 laps and we've won $50,000 for the pole and $50,000 for the segment. Hmmm, that makes $3,000 every 1.5 miles. I could get used to this!"

Mark Martin was right behind Irvan, with Wallace third, ahead of Elliott and Earnhardt.

The start of the second segment was, to no one's surprise, inverted following a fan vote, meaning Earnhardt would start 15th for the second 30 laps. Kyle Petty's hopes for victory ended after 30 laps with engine failure.

It didn't take long for the second segment to get interesting. On the second lap, Harry Gant and Michael Waltrip tangled. Jimmy Hensley, Dale Jarrett and Marlin all got a piece of the action, ending their hopes.

Mast took command, and went on to handle the pack to win the second segment and clinch the inside front-row position for the final 10-lap shootout. Earnhardt, who had fought his way up from the 15th-starting position, was on Mast's outside for the final start.

Into the first turn they went, and when Mast cut the wheel to the left, his Skoal Ford carried up the track and hit Earnhardt. Martin spurted to the lead, and it looked like he would pull away to win. He had the car and had proved it twice, coming from 14th to second in the first 30 laps and then from 18th to third in the second 30 laps. He stretched the lead and looked home-free until Terry Labonte crashed on the eighth lap of the 10-lap final.

Because of the special rules of The Winston, the final 10 laps must be green-flag laps, and scoring reverts to the last completed green flag lap when a yellow occurs.

As they lined up for the restart, Martin was on the inside, with Earnhardt on the outside. And as they came out of the fourth turn, Earnhardt jumped the green flag. NASCAR immediately dropped a yellow to create a new and fairer restart.

The field re-formed and when the green dropped again, Earnhardt and Martin were side-by-side in the battle for the victory. They remained side-by-side through the first and second turns, then down the backstretch. Earnhardt dove just a bit deeper into the outside of the third turn, and cleared Martin as they exited the fourth turn

Rick Mast and Dale Earnhardt commanded the front as the field lined up for the start of the final segment of The Winston.

The whole crew of the Goodwrench Lumina head to victory lane after winning The Winston.

to take the white flag. He maintained his advantage through the final 1.5 miles and then celebrated in victory lane.

Earnhardt had won his third The Winston trophy and collected $222,500 in the process, leaving Martin to the runner-up check of $102,500. Irvan was third, collecting $150,000 for 70 laps, while Ken Schrader battled his way into The Winston and then climbed through the field to finish fourth. Geoff Bodine finished fifth.

The teams would be at Charlotte for another full week. There would be plenty of time for those who had lost to recoup in time for the Coca-Cola 600 the following Sunday.

THE WINSTON

FINAL RESULTS

Fin. Pos.	Str. Pos.	Driver	Team	Fin. Pos.	Str. Pos.	Driver	Team
1	3	Dale Earnhardt	GM Goodwrench Chevrolet	11	20	Rick Mast	Wilco/Skoal Classic Racing Ford
2	14	Mark Martin	Valvoline Ford	12	9	Morgan Shepherd	Citgo Petroleum Corp. Ford
3	1	Ernie Irvan	Ernie Irvan	13	12	Harry Gant	Skoal Bandit Racing Chevrolet
4	17	Ken Schrader	Kodiak Chevrolet	14	4	Bill Elliott	Budweiser Ford
5	10	Geoff Bodine	Motorcraft Ford	15	13	Terry Labonte	Kellogg's Chevrolet
6	8	Darrell Waltrip	Western Auto Chevrolet	16	11	Ricky Rudd	Tide Chevrolet
7	16	Sterling Marlin	Raybestos Ford	17	15	Jimmy Hensley	Hanes Activewear Ford
8	2	Rusty Wallace	Miller Genuine Draft Pontiac	18	19	Michael Waltrip	Pennzoil Pontiac
9	5	Davey Allison	Texaco/Havoline Ford	19	7	Dale Jarrett	Interstate Batteries Chevrolet
10	18	Brett Bodine	Quaker State Ford	20	6	Kyle Petty	Mello Yello Pontiac

COCA-COLA 600

The excitement following The Winston had barely faded by the time the teams began preparation for the longest race of the season, the Coca-Cola 600 at Charlotte. There had been plenty of announcements to keep things lively. NASCAR, in a move aimed at helping teams control tire costs, had limited teams to three sets of Goodyears for practice and qualifying sessions. Mello Yello announced it had renewed its contract with Sabates Racing for an additional six years! Kodiak told the fans it would renew its sponsorship with Hendrick Motorsports for two more years.

Purolator said it would back the Kulwicki Racing team for three events. Ricky Rudd had told car owner Rick Hendrick he would not be back following this season, and instead, would form his own team beginning in 1994. Factory Stores Outlet Centers had replaced Carolina Pottery on the RahMoc Fords for Dick Trickle.

The stands were packed for the action-filled Coca-Cola 600.

Kenny Schrader won the pole and raced to a fourth place finish at Charlotte.

While all this was going on, it was "business as usual" in the garage area, and the black-clad Goodwrench crew coolly stared down those who raised any questions about driver Dale Earnhardt's victory under the Saturday night lights.

With the all-star race over, it was time to chase points again, and Earnhardt set about protecting his meager 20-point lead over Rusty Wallace.

When the evening qualifying session was completed, Brett Bodine stood in the garage, ruefully shaking his head.

"This is hard to believe. We came to Charlotte to sit on the pole for the Winston Open and missed by four-one hundredths of a second. Then we miss the pole for the 600 by exactly the same margin. It's just unbelievable," Bodine said.

The driver who beat him this time wasn't the DuPont Flash, but it was a Hendrick Motorsport team, with Kenny Schrader behind the wheel of the Kodiak Chevrolet.

Mark Martin, still smarting from his loss in The Winston, recovered and posted the third-fastest time of the day, just ahead of Rick Mast and Geoff Bodine. Michael Waltrip was a sparkling sixth with his Pennzoil Pontiac, breathing hope for a solid top-five finish into the yellow-suited team.

Sterling Marlin, Wallace, Rick Wilson and Jimmy Hensley completed the top ten.

Some big names missing, you noticed?

Earnhardt was 14th, Irvan 19th, Rudd 20th, Gordon 21st and Davey Allison a bewildered 23rd, not understanding why his Ford was more than three miles per hour off the pole speed. And if Davey was puzzled, think how Harry Gant (25th),

After winning the pole, Ken Schrader shares a proud moment with Hendrick Motorsport owner Rick Hendrick.

Kyle Petty struggled throughout the 600. Although Mark Martin led early, he also struggled, coming home with a 28th-place finish.

Geoff Bodine qualified fifth, but brought his Motorcraft Ford home 10th.

Hut Stricklin (26th), Bill Elliott (30th), Darrell Waltrip (31st), Dale Jarrett (32nd), and Kyle Petty (35th) felt. What was going on here, anyway?

Sunday's race had extra importance for Jarrett and Irvan. The Coca-Cola 600 is the third round counting towards the Winston Million, and each had a shot at the $100,000 bonus, if they could win the race. It was their last chance at the $1 million. Both had to win the 600 to carry any hopes to September and the Mountain Dew Southern 500. A loss here ended any chance of the huge bonus.

Sunday's start was the first for a 600 that would begin in the afternoon and end after darkness fell at Charlotte.

The teams had been waiting for a week for another shot at the black Chevrolet. Dale knew it—and understood he would have to have an exceptional day to win again on the 1.5-mile superspeedway.

Little did he know what would be in store

when the flag dropped on the 4:30 p.m. start of the 400-lapper.

Schrader, Martin and Geoff Bodine started the tussle right from the start, sharing the lead for the first 47 laps before Irvan joined the fun at the front. By quarter-distance, Earnhardt had grunted his way to the point where he fought with Irvan for the next 100 laps.

But on lap 221, Earnhardt was hit with a 15-second penalty for entering pit road on a green flag stop at a speed higher than the limit posted by NASCAR for the race. It cost him a lap, but on the restart on lap 229, he jumped past Jarrett and rookie Bobby Labonte to get back to the tail of the lead lap. He fought as hard as he could—and 100 laps later, although he had made up a half-lap and was second, he still trailed Jarrett.

Then Greg Sacks spun, the yellow came out, and Earnhardt made up his lap. He headed for pit road—and was penalized after NASCAR determined he had been the cause of Sacks' spin.

He was again a lap down.

On the restart, he and Jimmy Spencer blasted past leader Labonte, and when Rusty crunched his Miller Pontiac into the wall with 50 laps to go, Earnhardt was able to make up his second lap.

While Earnhardt was struggling to make up his laps, it looked like Dale Jarrett was on his way to a second victory towards the Million. But when the black Chevrolet got back on equal terms, the opinion of the crowd in the stands was that Earnhardt would not be denied.

The final restart came with Irvan at the point, followed by Martin, Schrader, Bobby Labonte, Jarrett, the DuPont Flash and Spencer. Earnhardt was lined up eighth, with Bill Elliott in the final car on the lead lap.

Martin's engine blew on the restart and headed for the garage. Seven laps later, Earnhardt whipped under Irvan for the lead and he merely left the others battling for what they could salvage.

This race was his, and there was no question about it. Penalties or not, the black Chevrolet was headed for victory lane for the first time since Dar-

lington in April.

Earnhardt ended Irvan and Jarrett's hopes for the Winston Million. Instead, now the two would have to battle Earnhardt at Darlington for the $100,000 consolation prize—a possibility neither had wanted to face.

The win, coupled with Wallace's wreck, gained Earnhardt 109 points in the championship race. He now led by 129.

Jeff Gordon won the four-way Chevrolet duel for second place, easing home ahead of Jarrett and Schrader, with Irvan making it a "first-five" for the Bowtie Brigade.

Elliott was the first Ford to finish, taking sixth, ahead of Jimmy Spencer and Bobby Labonte, the remaining cars on the lead lap.

Jarrett moved into third in the point standings, 79 points behind Wallace, while Geoff Bodine, Kyle Petty and Davey Allison were separated by only ten points for fourth, fifth and sixth place.

The Charlotte enduro was over. After two weeks in the same place, the teams were itching for a chance to try another track. The sun-soaked sauna at Dover and its Monster Mile were next.

Rusty Wallace's crew continued to scorch the competition on pit road.

He had to battle back from two separate penalties, but Dale Earnhardt found a way to win in front of his home crowd.

There were two great weekends at Charlotte for Dale Earnhardt, who also claimed the Coca-Cola 600 crown.

Fin. Pos.	Str. Pos.	Driver	Team	Fin. Pos.	Str. Pos.	Driver	Team
1	14	Dale Earnhardt	GM Goodwrench Chevrolet	22	37	Mike Wallace	Duron Paints Pontiac
2	21	Jeff Gordon	DuPont Auto Finishes Chevrolet	23	24	Kenny Wallace	Dirt Devil Pontiac
3	32	Dale Jarrett	Interstate Batteries Chevrolet	24	7	Sterling Marlin	Raybestos Brakes Ford
4	1	Ken Schrader	Kodiak Chevrolet	25	39	Jimmy Horton	Active Trucking Chevrolet
5	19	Ernie Irvan	Kodak Film Chevrolet	26	18	Ted Musgrave	Jasper Engines Ford
6	30	Bill Elliott	Budweiser Ford	27	15	Lake Speed	Purex Ford
7	27	Jimmy Spencer	Meineke Mufflers Ford	28	3	Mark Martin	Valvoline Ford
8	13	Bobby Labonte	Maxwell House Ford	29	8	Rusty Wallace	Miller Genuine Draft Pontiac
9	12	Morgan Shepherd	Citgo Ford	30	23	Davey Allison	Havoline Ford
10	5	Geoff Bodine	Motorcraft Ford	31	4	Rick Mast	Skoal Classic Ford
11	31	Darrell Waltrip	Western Auto Chevrolet	32	9	Rick Wilson	STP Pontiac
12	22	Phil Parsons	Manheim Auctions Chevrolet	33	29	Terry Labonte	Kellogg's Chevrolet
13	6	Michael Waltrip	Pennzoil Pontiac	34	38	Chad Little	Orkin Ford
14	35	Kyle Petty	Mello Yello Pontiac	35	40	Joe Ruttman	Fina Lube Ford
15	10	Jimmy Hensley	Hanes Activewear Ford	36	16	Derrike Cope	Bojangles' Ford
16	28	Bobby Hillin	Heilig-Meyers Ford	37	20	Ricky Rudd	Tide Chevrolet
17	11	Greg Sacks	Country Time Ford	38	33	Jimmy Means	Hurley Limo Ford
18	25	Harry Gant	Skoal Bandit Chevrolet	39	41	Dave Marcis	Pronto Auto Parts Chevrolet
19	36	Dick Trickle	Factory Stores Ford	40	17	Wally Dallenbach	Keystone Beer Ford
20	26	Hut Stricklin	McDonald's Ford	41	2	Brett Bodine	Quaker State Ford
21	34	Rich Bickle	Kraft Bull's-Eye BBQ Ford				

BUDWEISER 500

**DOVER DOWNS
INTERNATIONAL RACEWAY**

JUNE 6, 1993

Following his triumphant two weeks in his hometown Charlotte, Dale Earnhardt arrived at Dover Downs and its Monster Mile back in the place where he feels most comfortable—the lead in the NASCAR Winston Cup points table.

His two wins at Charlotte hadn't been easy—the victory in The Winston was controversial at best—and the win in the Coca-Cola 600 had been one he had to fight for, coming back after penalties.

So, to arrive at Dover's mile with a comfortable cushion over Rusty Wallace in the points table, thanks mostly to Rusty's engine failure at Charlotte, made a visit to the Delaware capitol a pleasant experience.

Goodyear had brought the tire it used at Bristol earlier in the year to Dover—and management had not put any sealer on the roller-coaster of a race track. The result?

A total of 25 drivers hammered the old track record into oblivion, with Ernie Irvan slapping his Kodak Chevrolet on the pole with a "Come and Get Me" lap more than 3.5 miles per hour faster than the old mark set by Mark Martin back in 1988!

Driver after driver turned track-record times—and still found themselves short of Irvan's 151.5 mph mark. In fact, five of the drivers who ran faster than the old mark had to come back for second round qual-

Davey Allison started third and finished third in the grinder at Dover.

Felix Sabates, owner of Kyle Petty's Mello Yello Pontiac and Kenny Wallace's Dirt Devil Pontiac, watches his cars circulate at Dover.

96

ifying. Their laps, despite being quicker than the old record, weren't fast enough to make the field on the first day!

It was a rousing qualifying session, and when it was over, Brett Bodine was the second-fastest, but was more than a mile per hour slower than the yellow Chevrolet.

Davey Allison was on track, qualifying third-fastest, with Wallace outside his right-hand door. Rick Wilson was a surprising fifth-quick, alongside Derrike Cope, returning to the site of his 1990 victory.

Kyle Petty lined up seventh, and right beside the Mello Yello Pontiac was the point-leader, with

either brief or easy about them. Drivers and crews know they are in for a long and extremely difficult afternoon—and the track, located close to the Atlantic Ocean, turns into a sweat-soaked adventure for the near-five hour event.

The race immediately took the tone of "anyone's show" and within the first 35 laps, Allison, Brett, Dave Marcis and Earnhardt had all taken their turn at the point.

An event record (and Delaware state record) 86,000 had packed their way into Dennis McGlynn's place, and before they went home, all would have agreed they had seen quite a show—and gotten their money's worth.

Dave Marcis put his Chevrolet on the point early in the Dover race, but later was involved in a wreck that ended his day.

the black Chevrolet nearly two miles per hour slower in qualifying than Irvan. Ford drivers Mark Martin and Geoff Bodine completed the top-10 qualifiers.

Dover would prove to be as exciting a race as usual, if the pre-race line-up had anything to do with it. Among the drivers who would have to fight their way to the front of the field included Terry Labonte, Darrell Waltrip, Sterling Marlin, Jeff Gordon, Dale Jarrett, Michael Waltrip and Dick Trickle.

Dover's races are "grinders." There is nothing

Earnhardt proved early that he had a car capable of winning but he cut a tire while leading and lost a lap on pit road having the tire replaced.

Earnhardt got his lap back after Ricky Rudd smacked the first turn wall to bring out the fifth yellow of the race.

Earnhardt cut a second tire on lap 280, while running second on the track. The Goodwrench Chevrolet driver again hit pit road and lost a lap.

That stop put him out of sequence with the remainder of the drivers, and when they cycled through green flag stops, Earnhardt was once

Inside Dover's "Monster Mile" is a horse-racing track which offers fans excellent vantage points.

again in the lead, and boosted his margin to more than 10 seconds over Rusty with just over 315 laps completed.

Earnhardt watched that hard-fought lead disappear when Stricklin spun on the back stretch, bringing out yet another of the event's record 14 yellow flags.

But from then on, the race was Earnhardt's to lose—and he had no intentions of letting a trophy from the Monster Mile get away. He led all but one of the final 154 laps—and backed off toward the end of the race to conserve his tires in case someone made a run at him in the final laps of the race.

A charge by Dale Jarrett cut the gap, and with two laps to go, it looked like Jarrett might have something for Earnhardt. But the five-time champion just eased his way to a four-car-length victory in a race that took nearly four hours and 45 minutes to complete.

Allison was the third car across the line, with six drivers on the lead lap at the end of the marathon. Martin finished fourth, with Ken Schrader fifth. Rick Mast completed the top six. Harry Gant beat Jimmy Spencer for seventh place, a lap down, with Morgan Shepherd and Bobby Hamilton completing the top 10.

Wallace's hot streak of three victories was truly over. And his hopes of racing Earnhardt for the championship took a second-straight serious hit when the Miller Pontiac driver and Mark Martin's Valvoline Ford collided in the fourth turn with less than 75 laps remaining.

Wallace slammed the outside wall, ending the Pontiac's day. The wreck also sent Jimmy Hensley and Geoff Bodine to an early shower.

Others eliminated from the race after being involved in "entanglements" with the Dover concrete included Kyle Petty, Dave Marcis, Cope,

The battle for Dover was fought among Dale Earnhardt, Mark Martin and Dale Jarrett. Jarrett got past Martin for second at the end.

Marlin, Rudd, P.J. Jones, Phil Parsons and Greg Sacks, named to drive the Country Time Ford for the remainder of the season with the exception of Watkins Glen.

As Earnhardt headed back to North Carolina, he took a moment to savor the 109-point lead he had built over Wallace in the last two point races. But he wasted no more than a moment.

He knew very well that this championship was not over—he had seen the point lead come and go and then return in the span of just the last few races. Dover may have been the 12th race of the season—but there were 18 events remaining. There was a long road yet to travel.

Ernie Irvan gets service for his Kodak Chevrolet on Dover's tight pit road. Irvan later left the race due to engine failure.

Dale and Teresa Earnhardt share yet another victory lane with Miss Winston after Dale's Dover win.

Fin. Pos.	Str. Pos.	Driver	Team	Fin. Pos.	Str. Pos.	Driver	Team
1	8	Dale Earnhardt	GM Goodwrench Chevrolet	20	26	Terry Labonte	Kellogg's Chevrolet
2	29	Dale Jarrett	Interstate Batteries Chevrolet	21	4	Rusty Wallace	Miller Genuine Draft Pontiac
3	3	Davey Allison	Havoline Ford	22	11	Jimmy Hensley	Matchbox Toys Ford
4	9	Mark Martin	Valvoline Ford	23	10	Geoff Bodine	Motorcraft Ford
5	12	Ken Schrader	Kodiak Chevrolet	24	28	Darrell Waltrip	Western Auto Chevrolet
6	23	Rick Mast	Skoal Classic Ford	25	30	Bobby Hillin	Heilig-Meyers Ford
7	13	Harry Gant	Skoal Bandit Chevrolet	26	38	Jimmy Means	Hurley Limo Ford
8	20	Jimmy Spencer	Meineke Mufflers Ford	27	31	Michael Waltrip	Pennzoil Pontiac
9	16	Morgan Shepherd	Citgo Ford	28	34	Dick Trickle	Carolina Pottery Ford
10	33	Bobby Hamilton	Holgate Toys Ford	29	7	Kyle Petty	Mello Yello Pontiac
11	5	Rick Wilson	STP Pontiac	30	17	Lake Speed	Purex Ford
12	32	Wally Dallenbach	Keystone Beer Ford	31	6	Derrike Cope	Bojangles' Ford
13	35	Kenny Wallace	Dirt Devil Pontiac	32	1	Ernie Irvan	Kodak Film Chevrolet
14	25	Ted Musgrave	Jasper Engines Ford	33	22	Sterling Marlin	Raybestos Ford
15	37	Hut Stricklin	McDonald's Ford	34	36	P.J. Jones	Melling Auto Products Ford
16	2	Brett Bodine	Quaker State Ford	35	15	Ricky Rudd	Tide Chevrolet
17	24	Bill Elliott	Budweiser Ford	36	18	Dave Marcis	Swanson Foods Chevrolet
18	21	Jeff Gordon	DuPont Auto Finishes Chevrolet	37	14	Phil Parsons	Manheim Auctions Chevrolet
19	19	Bobby Labonte	Maxwell House Ford	38	27	Greg Sacks	Country Time Ford

CHAMPION SPARK PLUG 500

Kyle Petty's day at Dover may have come to a premature end when he was involved in a mid-race wreck, but it merely gave him a few more hours to anticipate the upcoming junket he would make in the days between the Budweiser 500 and the Champion Spark Plug 500.

Petty has long been a Harley-Davidson fan, and has owned his own "Hog" for some time. He's such a buff that he bought The King one for Christmas, and Richard has been seen tooling around the roads near his shop over the past year, helmet covering those trademark wrap-around shades.

When the checkered fell at Dover, and the group finally was able to fight its way clear of the enormous crowd, Kyle and crew chief Robin Pemberton, along with a pair of friends, mounted the Hogs and set off on a 1700-mile journey that concluded with the opening of practice at the Mattioli's 2.5-mile superspeedway.

In the intervening days, the four rode their Harleys to New York City, where they spent the night at the Plaza Hotel. Then they were off to Portland, ME, and on to Louden, NH, for a test session at the New Hampshire track in preparation for the upcoming race there. From there they went to Pemberton's home-town of Saratoga Springs, NY, before heading for Pocono.

Kyle Petty was strong throughout the day at Pocono, notching a five-second victory over pole-sitter Kenny Schrader.

Michael Waltrip found a quiet moment before the start of the race with Elizabeth "Buffy" Franks, to whom he had proposed in victory lane after he won the April Busch race. She said yes!

After a sixth-place start, Brett Bodine's day ended early with a broken timing chain.

One of the most interesting aspects of the trip was the homemade video Kyle shot along the way with his trusty handy-cam. Everywhere the group went, they recorded their trip, including interviews with people they met in highway rest stops to the doorman at the Plaza.

Kyle was full of stories when he arrived at the converted spinach farm, but when it came time for qualifying, Kenny Schrader had the way to put an end to "Travels with Kyle."

Schrader set a new lap record at the triangular track, beating Mark Martin for the fastest lap by an infinitesimal .096 of a second. The pole was Schrader's third of the young season.

Hut Stricklin took his McDonald's Ford from the outhouse to the penthouse. After having to take a provisional start the previous weekend at Dover just to get in the field, Stricklin blistered Pocono with a lap good enough for the third-fastest spot at the end of the day.

Jeff Gordon put up some good numbers to start outside Stricklin, and point-leader Dale Earnhardt proved to the field once again that he was on the championship track. He would start fifth for Sunday's 200-lapper, alongside Brett Bodine, who

continued his outstanding string of qualifying performances.

Davey Allison was dialed in, and would start the race on the inside of the row that contained the well-traveled Petty. Jimmy Spencer and Rusty Wallace completed the top-10.

Once again, there were several normal front-runners who would have to fight their way from the back of the field. Dale Jarrett, Derrike Cope, Morgan Shepherd, Harry Gant, Michael Waltrip, Terry Labonte, Sterling Marlin and Darrell Waltrip all turned in "off" qualifying performances and would start the race from the second half of the field.

When it's your turn to win on the NASCAR Winston Cup circuit, there is little anyone can do about it. Dale Earnhardt had come back from laps down in each of the previous two races to win. This week, it was Kyle's turn—and he didn't have to fight his way through the problems like Earnhardt had.

Instead, Kyle treated Pocono like he has treated Rockingham in the past—taking the lead easily, building large margins over his competitors, watching those leads disappear via caution flags, and then dominating on his way to victory.

That was the story of the Champion Spark Plug 500 at Pocono.

When the totals were tallied at the end, Kyle had led seven times for 148 of the 200 laps and beat second-place Schrader by nearly five seconds in a sparkling performance.

The only time the outcome seemed in doubt was in the final 20 laps when Kyle pitted for new Goodyear Eagles during the last caution and came out fourth behind Shepherd, Marlin and Rudd, who had not pitted.

Within five laps, Kyle had blasted to the point and pulled away for his first win since last August at Watkins Glen.

Finishing behind Schrader were Gant, Spencer and a flashy Ted Musgrave, having one of his better races of the season. Davey Allison was a solid

Dale Earnhardt's crew goes under the hood for hasty repairs during a yellow flag. They were successful in keeping Dale on the lead lap, where he finished 11th.

Richard Petty watches as driver Rick Wilson drives to a 12th-place finish.

sixth followed by Shepherd, Marlin, Rudd and Bill Elliott. Dale Earnhardt was 11th, the final car on the lead lap despite a persistent oil leak.

As Petty clambered out of his car in victory lane, he had his handy-cam cranked and rolling. As he stood on the top of his Pontiac in celebration, his video camera recorded the excitement of the crowd—and proved a fitting ending to the 1700-mile odyssey that had begun the previous week at Dover.

And after the race was over, Kyle quietly talked of what winning this particular race meant to him.

"This was the last race that Alan won, and he rode home on our plane with us that night," Kyle said. "He rode home with us a lot and he, Felix and I were good friends. We did a lot of things no one knew about and when he won the race, it made it a long ride, because he'd constantly let you know WHO won the race—and WHO didn't!

"We went back a long ways together. We argued a lot together. But we were good friends. He made fun of me, my long hair and my earring. I made fun of him and his short hair and his ever-present comb.

"So to come back here and win the last race he won a year later is, and always will be, very special to me."

Although Earnhardt suffered with the oil leak, he added points to his lead. And the season began to look like it was all over for Rusty Wallace. For the third-straight race, the Miller Pontiac made an early exit.

This time Wallace completed only four laps before the engine failed, and the 1989 Winston Cup Champion headed for the garage. He was classified 39th and fell all the way to fifth in the standings. Three races ago, after Sears Point, he led by 20. Now he was 298 behind.

Allison's sixth place boosted him into the challenger's position in the point standings, but he was 125 points behind Earnhardt.

This day, the points didn't really matter to Davey. He was still riding the high from the night before, when the Allison family was presented the "Bill France Award" by the Mattioli family. The award is presented to the person or company who has made a significant contribution to the sport·of NASCAR Winston Cup racing and to Pocono Raceway.

Dale Jarrett continued to hang in a contender's spot, now third in the point standings, just 22 points behind Allison. Kyle jumped to fourth in the standings on the strength of his victory.

Darrell Waltrip's Western Auto team suffered a frustrating afternoon after Darrell went out due to engine failure.

Petty and his friends loaded their Harleys in the Mello Yello transporter. Their mid-summer jaunt was nothing but a video memory now, but for Kyle, it had ended in the most pleasant way.

This was a victory he would treasure.

Kyle Petty celebrated his victory by using his video camera to tape the crowd's reaction to his win.

Fin. Pos.	Str. Pos.	Driver	Team	Fin. Pos.	Str. Pos.	Driver	Team
1	8	Kyle Petty	Mello Yello Pontiac	21	27	Michael Waltrip	Pennzoil Pontiac
2	1	Ken Schrader	Kodiak Chevrolet	22	37	Jimmy Means	Hurley Limo Ford
3	26	Harry Gant	Skoal Bandit Chevrolet	23	33	Dave Marcis	Marcis Racing Chevrolet
4	9	Jimmy Spencer	Meineke Mufflers Ford	24	14	Geoff Bodine	Motorcraft Ford
5	15	Ted Musgrave	Jasper Engines Ford	25	20	Wally Dallenbach	Keystone Beer Ford
6	7	Davey Allison	Havoline Ford	26	38	Kerry Teague	Linro Chevrolet
7	25	Morgan Shepherd	Citgo Ford	27	11	Lake Speed	Purex Ford
8	32	Sterling Marlin	Raybestos Ford	28	4	Jeff Gordon	DuPont Auto Finishes Chevrolet
9	12	Ricky Rudd	Tide Chevrolet	29	6	Brett Bodine	Quaker State Ford
10	16	Bill Elliott	Budweiser Ford	30	34	Darrell Waltrip	Western Auto Chevrolet
11	5	Dale Earnhardt	GM Goodwrench Chevrolet	31	2	Mark Martin	Valvoline Ford
12	22	Rick Wilson	STP Pontiac	32	30	Terry Labonte	Kellogg's Chevrolet
13	3	Hut Stricklin	McDonald's Ford	33	24	Derrike Cope	Bojangles' Ford
14	28	Phil Parsons	Manheim Auctions Chevrolet	34	17	Ernie Irvan	Kodak Film Chevrolet
15	31	Kenny Wallace	Dirt Devil Pontiac	35	39	Trevor Boys	Rumple Furniture Pontiac
16	13	Rick Mast	Skoal Classic Ford	36	35	Dick Trickle	Factory Stores of America Ford
17	18	Jimmy Hensley	Matchbox Toys Ford	37	36	Jimmy Horton	Active Trucking Chevrolet
18	29	Greg Sacks	Country Time Ford	38	19	Bobby Hillin	Heilig-Meyers Ford
19	21	Dale Jarrett	Interstate Batteries Chevrolet	39	10	Rusty Wallace	Miller Genuine Draft Pontiac
20	23	Bobby Labonte	Maxwell House Ford	40	40	Graham Taylor	State Shuttle Ford

MILLER GENUINE DRAFT 400

One could excuse the weariness noted in the NASCAR Winston Cup truck drivers, crew members and drivers. The Miller Genuine Draft 400 marked the sixth race in as many weeks for the teams, and the rigs had made round-trips to California, Delaware, Pennsylvania and now Michigan in the last few weeks. The only respite had been the fortnight at Charlotte, and in many ways, that had been just as wearying as a road trip for the teams.

Finally, they could see the light at the end of the current travel tunnel, the worst physical hammering they would take this year.

Rudd stretches his lead during the final laps on his way to victory.

Ricky Rudd beat Hendrick Motorsport teammate
Jeff Gordon to notch his 14th career victory.

Ricky and Linda Rudd enjoy their first victory lane visit of the season with Miss Winston after Rudd won by becoming a gas miser.

Sure, there was a seven-week foray on the agenda beginning with Bristol, but the majority of those races were close to home.

Michigan marked the end of the string, and no one was happier than the truck drivers.

Roger Penske's sanitary two-mile oval is always one of the favorite tracks on the tour for competitors. Not only is it sparkling clean, but everything is as organized as it can be. The garage area is more than roomy—in fact, the 18-wheel rigs appear at times to get lost in the paved expanse. There is never a problem with having room to back out of the garages—there's plenty of room for access, egress and the crews. And the folks who work for general manager Gene Haskett are as friendly as can be.

With nearly half of the season on the books, Dale Earnhardt cruised into MIS with plenty of points in hand over new second-place point-holder Davey Allison. No one had to tell Earnhardt or any of the other General Motors drivers how important the races at Michigan are. This is home turf for the manufacturers, and the execs turn out on Sunday to watch "their" teams perform. A win here can go a long way toward making late-season negotiations a pleasant experience!

Brett Bodine had been knocking on the door of a pole for the first third of the season, and headed for Michigan, he had started from the outside pole at Bristol, Charlotte and Dover. It was only a matter of time until he posted the quickest qualifying lap—and no one was happier when he did it at Michigan than the Ford folks. It was a solid start to the weekend for the Blue Oval bunch.

Chevrolet executives were reasonably pleased as well. Ricky Rudd had slapped his Tide Chevrolet on the outside pole, just ahead of Davey Allison and Kenny Schrader. Chevy-driving Ernie Irvan and Dale Earnhardt claimed the third row, with Mark Martin and a surprising Lake Speed making up the fourth row. Rick Mast was ninth, and Michael Waltrip became the fastest Pontiac driver, qualifying tenth. Junior Johnson's cars, with Bill Elliott 11th and Hut Stricklin 12th, made up the next row.

Qualifying wasn't without its dramas, however, when Harry Gant was forced to a back-up car after his primary Chevrolet was damaged in an altercation with the Michigan concrete wall. And Allison's lap came with his race engine after his team found an oil leak in the qualifying engine.

Rudd used the Michigan forum to talk in general terms about the team he would form for the 1994 season, and announced that Tide would accompany him in his new role as a car owner and

driver. Although he did not announce which nameplate his cars would carry next year, he made it clear that his primary focus for the remainder of this year was to win races for Tide and the Hendrick Motorsports team for which he drove. Starting from the front row, he hoped that Michigan would turn out to be a victory for him. The only other time he started from the front row, a few weeks ago at Sears Point, he had come home third, his best finish of the young season.

After Rudd led the first nine laps, it wasn't long before Dale Earnhardt and Mark Martin charged to the front to show that they had cars capable of taking charge of the race. And as the race wore on toward the half-way mark, it became obvious that Martin had the car best suited to Michigan that afternoon.

With less than 40 laps remaining in the race, Martin was so strong that others had concluded that if the race ran green the remainder of the way, they would all be fighting for second and third place.

Except for Rudd. Knowing he had a second- or third-place car, at best, his only way to victory lane was through fuel consumption. He would have to run 54 laps on one tank of Unocal if he was to win—if the race stayed green. So Ricky began the gamble, easing in and out of the throttle and hoping the others would have to pit for fuel.

With 17 laps left, the first of the front-running pack made his stop, with Bill Elliott on pit road. Eight laps later, Sterling Marlin took his Ford in for fuel and leader Martin ran out of gas on the backstretch. He coasted to pit road for fuel.

Rudd swept into the lead with just nine laps to go, wondering if Morgan Shepherd could make the distance. The Citgo Ford driver couldn't.

And just as Rudd was rehearsing his victory lane speech, he looked in the mirror to find Hendrick Motorsport teammate Jeff Gordon beginning to loom large.

Gordon had chopped the distance and closed on Rudd, leaving Ricky no choice but to get back to work, hoping he had conserved enough fuel to give him a working margin.

The Virginian worked his lead to just more than a second, and then came home the winner for the 14th time in his Winston Cup career.

It was his first trip to the winner's circle since Dover last year and he could not have been more delighted. He had beaten the odds, taking a less-competitive car to victory lane by shrewdly using everything available to him —including out-thinking his faster rivals.

Gordon's runner-up position matched his career best at Charlotte, while Ernie Irvan, Dale Jarrett and Rusty Wallace completed the top-five.

Where were the point leaders? Earnhardt finished 14th, a lap down after handling problems. Fuel mileage also hurt the Goodwrench Chevrolet driver, since he was unable to complete the last long run under green without stopping.

Allison was taken out of the running when hit in an early-race wreck. He returned to the fray after it took his team more than 60 laps to repair damage from the crash. He was classified 35th and fell to sixth place in the point standings.

Brett Bodine, who had such high hopes after winning his first pole of the year, headed for the garage after just 22 laps when his Ernie Elliott-built engine gave up the ghost for the day.

After three-straight poor finishes, Rusty Wallace stopped the streak with his fifth-place finish. He ran the last 51 laps under green—and ran out of fuel when he came out of the fourth corner with the checkered flag in sight. The gamble by crew chief Buddy Parrott helped Wallace move from fifth in the standings back to third.

Dale Jarrett emerged in second place in the points, 213 behind Earnhardt. Wallace now trailed by 269 and was just 11 points ahead of fourth-place Kyle Petty.

As they loaded their mounts, no team breathed a sigh of relief louder than the Goodwrench crew. They had entered this string second place in the point standings, and after racing from coast-to-coast, they had built a 200-plus point lead. A weekend off would be a welcome relief before everyone returned to the pressure cooker with the Pepsi 400 at Daytona Beach.

Brett Bodine's pole position didn't last long. He went out of the race after 22 laps with engine failure.

NASCAR Winston Cup races at Michigan always draw sell-out crowds.

Mark Martin and Jack Roush talk race strategy. Mark qualified seventh and finished sixth after being a factor throughout the day.

Fin. Pos.	Str. Pos.	Driver	Team	Fin. Pos.	Str. Pos.	Driver	Team
1	2	Ricky Rudd	Tide Chevrolet	22	34	Greg Sacks	Country Time Ford
2	23	Jeff Gordon	DuPont Auto Finishes Chevrolet	23	26	Jimmy Hensley	Matchbox Toys Ford
3	5	Ernie Irvan	Kodak Film Chevrolet	24	36	Dave Marcis	Marcis Racing Chevrolet
4	17	Dale Jarrett	Interstate Batteries Chevrolet	25	27	Wally Dallenbach	Keystone Beer Ford
5	15	Rusty Wallace	Miller Genuine Draft Pontiac	26	39	Jim Sauter	Pedigree Chevrolet
6	7	Mark Martin	Valvoline Ford	27	30	Derrike Cope	Bojangles' Ford
7	13	Morgan Shepherd	Citgo Ford	28	41	Jimmy Means	Hurley Limo Ford
8	12	Sterling Marlin	Raybestos Ford	29	33	Kenny Wallace	Dirt Devil Pontiac
9	11	Bill Elliott	Budweiser Ford	30	8	Lake Speed	Purex Ford
10	37	Harry Gant	Skoal Bandit Chevrolet	31	35	Dick Trickle	Factory Stores of America Ford
11	9	Rick Mast	Skoal Classic Ford	32	40	H.B. Bailey	Almeda Auto Parts Pontiac
12	29	Kyle Petty	Mello Yello Pontiac	33	31	Bobby Hillin	Heilig-Meyers Ford
13	28	Phil Parsons	Manheim Auctions Chevrolet	34	24	Rick Wilson	STP Pontiac
14	6	Dale Earnhardt	GM Goodwrench Chevrolet	35	3	Davey Allison	Havoline Ford
15	32	Ted Musgrave	Jasper Engines Ford	36	19	Bobby Labonte	Maxwell House Ford
16	4	Ken Schrader	Kodiak Chevrolet	37	10	Michael Waltrip	Pennzoil Pontiac
17	18	Geoff Bodine	Motorcraft Ford	38	22	P.J. Jones	Melling Auto Products Ford
18	21	Jimmy Spencer	Meineke Mufflers Ford	39	1	Brett Bodine	Quaker State Ford
19	14	Darrell Waltrip	Western Auto Chevrolet	40	38	Clay Young	Means Racing Ford
20	25	Terry Labonte	Kellogg's Chevrolet	41	20	Jimmy Horton	Active Trucking Chevrolet
21	16	Hut Stricklin	McDonald's Ford				

PEPSI 400

A s Richard Childress' crew loaded the pair of Goodwrench Chevrolets into the back of the transporter for the trip from Welcome, NC, to Daytona, there were some light-hearted moments. After all, there was a 200-plus point lead in hand, and everyone remembered how good the cars had been at Daytona in February. Despite the fact the team had come up just short of winning the Daytona 500 by STP, they had been the class of the field for the entire Speedweeks at The Beach. There was no reason the team should have any less confidence as it headed for the annual July 400-miler.

Just 60 miles up the road, crew chief Ray Evernham and his mates were pushing the two Chevrolets prepared for the DuPont

No matter what time of the year it is, Daytona always attracts an enormous crowd to its Winston Cup races.

Mike Beam, crew chief for Bill Elliott's Budweiser Ford, tried throughout the first half of the season to unlock the gate to victory lane, without success.

Flash onto their transporter. Like the black-clad Goodwrench team, they remembered how well Jeff Gordon had run in the February events at The Beach. And their hopes were that the youngster could run just four positions better than he had finished in the 500 and give the team a chance to visit its first real NASCAR Winston Cup victory lane.

Over the years, teams have used the July Daytona race as a vacation for crew members and their families. This time, there wouldn't be time for

that he had one of the most potent cars in the field. It was merely a matter of waiting long enough—and getting everything right—before Irvan would be the fastest qualifier at Daytona.

This weekend, it would be his turn.

His qualifying turn was well down the list—and he had plenty at which to shoot. Kyle Petty's Mello Yello Pontiac had been one of the quickest cars throughout practice and the third-generation driver was atop the list when Irvan pulled off pit road.

Just over 47 seconds later, Irvan had snaked the pole from Kyle and had to wait until the remaining teams took their best shots at unseating the yellow Chevrolet from its second pole of the season. None succeeded.

Derrike Cope and Dale Earnhardt battle for the lead early in the Pepsi 400. Earnhardt would win and Cope would finish 24th.

that. The New Hampshire date was the following weekend—and the team vacations would have to wait.

With Ricky Rudd forming his own team for the next season, and announcing he would field Fords with Tide's backing, Hendrick Motorsport wasted no time in naming Rudd's replacement in the "5" car for the coming season. Terry Labonte was named as the new Hendrick driver, immediately triggering speculation that Kellogg's would leave Billy Hagan's team with Labonte in the switch to the 5.

After winning three of the last four restrictor-plate races, Ernie Irvan had proven without doubt

Dale Earnhardt and Ernie Irvan listen as Tony Glover tells a "fish story" prior to the start of the Pepsi 400.

Pole-sitter Ernie Irvan leads the field to the green flag to start the Pepsi 400. Irvan would finish seventh.

So, it would be Ernie and Kyle on the front row, with Davey Allison and a surprising Derrike Cope making up the second row. The fourth-quickest time was one Cope didn't expect, particularly because Cope's qualifying motor burned a piston in practice and the team went to the truck and pulled off the Talladega race engine and stuffed it in the Bojangles' Ford.

Earnhardt proved his teammates had reason for their pre-event confidence. He was fifth-fastest, just ahead of Bill Elliott, who hoped the second half of the season would be a complete turnaround when compared to his dismal first half.

Harry Gant, Darrell Waltrip, Rick Wilson and Michigan winner Ricky Rudd completed the top-10 in qualifying.

As it seemed to be all year, the second half of the field would include some runners who would make things interesting when it came race time. Among those who came up short in qualifying were Geoff Bodine, Sterling Marlin, Jeff Gordon, Jimmy Spencer and Terry Labonte.

Once it began, the race turned quickly into a royal battle. As soon as one driver would get to the point, a pack would get together and draft by the leader. Time after time, Earnhardt went to the lead, and was displaced. Despite the 28 lead changes, Earnhardt proved time and again he had the desire—and the car—to win the race.

The last of the race's six cautions came out with just 12 laps remaining and with Earnhardt in the lead. When the green flag came out with eight laps left in the race, Earnhardt knew the pack behind him would give him no quarter. There were 19 cars on the lead lap—and every one was hunting his scalp.

The black Chevrolet was in the lead as the snarling pack came down to take the white flag lap, and as they headed into the first turn, Earnhardt's car slid a little high. As the cars came out of the second turn, Dale had to burp the gas. Schrader, who had climbed through the field to contend for the win, took his best shot on the outside of Earnhardt.

The five-time champion was not about to give

up easily. Earnhardt went on, as Sterling Marlin jumped alongside Schrader to battle for second place.

The white Chevrolet and the blue Ford raced side-by-side through the remainder of the lap, with Marlin just squeezing past Schrader at the line.

Rudd came home in fourth place, and Gordon repeated his Daytona 500 finish with a fifth.

Martin nipped Irvan for sixth place, with Jarrett right behind Irvan. Terry Labonte and Ted Musgrave completed the top ten.

The victory was Earnhardt's fourth of the year in a points race, and his fifth, including The Winston.

More importantly, with Rusty Wallace finishing 18th, it gave Earnhardt a commanding lead in the point standings.

With the season half over, Earnhardt now led Dale Jarrett by 231 points, and had sent Rusty back to the drawing board, 345 points in arrears.

Wallace may have been third, but he was a mere six points ahead of Morgan Shepherd, who quietly continued to put together a splendid season. Shepherd had nine top-10 finishes in the first 15 races of the season. Ken Schrader moved to fifth in the points while Kyle Petty was now sixth and Davey Allison seventh. Rookie Jeff Gordon was eighth in the point standings. Only 92 points separated third through eighth in the point ladder.

The first visit to the Bahre's New Hampshire Motor Speedway was next on the schedule.

After qualifying third, Davey Allison and his Havoline Ford had problems; he struggled to a 31st-place finish.

It may not have been the Daytona win Dale Earnhardt wanted, but he was delighted to score his fourth victory of the season.

Fin. Pos.	Str. Pos.	Driver	Team	Fin. Pos.	Str. Pos.	Driver	Team
1	5	Dale Earnhardt	GM Goodwrench Chevrolet	22	4	Michael Waltrip	Pennzoil Pontiac
2	22	Sterling Marlin	Raybestos Ford	23	33	Jeff Purvis	Phoenix Construction Chevrolet
3	41	Ken Schrader	Kodiak Chevrolet	24	4	Derrike Cope	Bojangles' Ford
4	10	Ricky Rudd	Tide Chevrolet	25	35	Phil Parsons	Manheim Auctions Chevrolet
5	27	Jeff Gordon	DuPont Auto Finishes Chevrolet	26	38	Dick Trickle	Factory Stores Ford
6	18	Mark Martin	Valvoline Ford	27	24	Dave Marcis	Raines Kennels Chevrolet
7	1	Ernie Irvan	Kodak Film Chevrolet	28	32	Kenny Wallace	Dirt Devil Pontiac
8	13	Dale Jarrett	Interstate Batteries Chevrolet	29	40	Loy Allen	Naturally Fresh Ford
9	31	Terry Labonte	Kellogg's Chevrolet	30	36	P.J. Jones	Melling Auto Products Ford
10	14	Ted Musgrave	Jasper Engines Ford	31	3	Davey Allison	Havoline Ford
11	9	Rick Wilson	STP Pontiac	32	37	Ritchie Petty	Winston Cup Water Ford
12	25	Bobby Hillin	Heilig-Meyers Ford	33	2	Kyle Petty	Mello Yello Pontiac
13	8	Darrell Waltrip	Western Auto Chevrolet	34	19	Jimmy Hensley	The Family Channel Ford
14	20	Morgan Shepherd	Citgo Ford	35	29	Wally Dallenbach	Keystone Beer Ford
15	23	Greg Sacks	Country Time Ford	36	34	Jimmy Means	NAPA Ford
16	12	Rick Mast	Skoal Classic Ford	37	21	Geoff Bodine	Motorcraft Ford
17	30	Bobby Hamilton	Fina Lube Ford	38	39	Jimmy Horton	Active Trucking Chevrolet
18	17	Rusty Wallace	Miller Genuine Draft Pontiac	39	28	Jimmy Spencer	Meineke Mufflers Ford
19	16	Brett Bodine	Quaker State Ford	40	15	Hut Stricklin	McDonald's Ford
20	6	Bill Elliott	Budweiser Ford	41	26	Bobby Labonte	Maxwell House Ford
21	7	Harry Gant	Skoal Bandit Chevrolet				

SLICK 50 300

*Huge flags welcomed both American
and Canadian NASCAR Winston Cup
fans at New Hampshire's
inaugural event.*

Normally, when a new event is added to the NASCAR Winston Cup series schedule, the hype around the event consumes any other news generated during that weekend.

When Sears Point, Phoenix and Watkins Glen joined the circuit in the late-80's, that was the case. The new markets responded to the series stars with voluminous publicity—and the fans responded in droves, making the events winners from the first time the green flag dropped.

The inaugural Slick 50 300 at New Hampshire was no different. Papers within a 100-mile radius of the track out-did themselves, almost in a conscious effort to make their coverage better than their competition's. Satellite television trucks were everywhere. It was a debut by which to gauge future events.

But there were other announcements that stole some of the headlines from New Hampshire's initial Winston Cup event.

Bahari Racing announced it had re-signed Michael Waltrip for three years, through the end of the 1996 season. Brett Bodine and Kenny Bernstein also announced they had renewed their contract for another season.

*Rusty Wallace returned to victory lane at New
Hampshire, earning his fifth victory of the season*

And Neil Bonnett announced he would return to the driver's seat for Talladega, two weeks hence, in a black Chevrolet entered by Richard Childress. Bonnett's mount would be the Chevrolet Dale Earnhardt drove to a second place in the Daytona 500 by STP. It would be Bonnett's first time in a Winston Cup car since Darlington in the TranSouth 500 in April, 1990. Bonnett had been working with Earnhardt and Childress testing Dale's Chevrolets at several tracks over the past few months. Bonnett stressed his "comeback" would, more than likely, be just the single race.

While all that was going on, little could take away from the culmination of a dream for Dick Bahre and his son, Gary. For years, Bahre had dreamed of a superspeedway in the Northeast, and after making his fortune in land development and banking in New Hampshire, Bahre bought the former Bryar Motorsports Park, and built the flat,

one-mile superspeedway on his own. Some $25 million later, the track was completed and opened for business.

He did it all without the guarantee of a date for a Winston Cup race from NASCAR, feeling, (if you'll excuse the phrase taken from "Field of Dreams,") that "if he built it, they would come."

Three years after his first NASCAR Busch Grand National race at the track, NASCAR Winston Cup competitors were lined up on pit road, ready to answer the green flag.

The only thing missing was defending champion Alan Kulwicki with his arm around the shoulders of Dick Bahre — two who worked against all odds to make their fondest dreams come true.

When the first qualifying session was completed, Fords had claimed the front row for the inaugural race. Mark Martin and Sterling Marlin emerged the fastest, with Hendrick Motorsport

The Valvoline Ford's crew was on top of everything throughout the race, keeping Mark within striking distance of Rusty Wallace.

Kenny Wallace's crew goes over the wall to service the Dirt Devil Pontiac.

teammates Jeff Gordon and Schrader making up the second row. Fifth-fastest was Terry Labonte, just ahead of BGN regular Jeff Burton, who would make his Winston Cup debut with a Thunderbird leased from Jack Roush by his Filmar BGN team.

Davey Allison and Ernie Irvan shared the fourth row, with Dale Jarrett and Ricky Rudd completing the top ten. Dale Earnhardt and Rusty Wallace had their problems in qualifying at the 1.058-mile track, with Earnhardt qualifying 24th and Wallace facing a long climb through the field from his 33rd starting position.

After the opening day hoopla in front of 66,000 fans, the field rolled out for the first Cup race in New England since 1970, when the late Bobby Isaac won in a Northern Tour race at Thompson, CT!

For nearly the first third of the 300-lap race, Martin and Marlin put their stamp on the event. The two led every lap until Allison emerged as a serious contender on lap 82.

Marlin returned to the front and looked like he might finally win his first Winston Cup race, lead-

Mark Martin led the field away from the green flag and would be a contender all day. He won a late-race battle with Davey Allison to finish second behind Rusty Wallace.

ing 123 of the first 160 laps, but faded from the lead after a bumping match with Earnhardt, who was trying to get a lost lap back. Earnhardt's transmission locked up during a pit stop.

And after the altercations that triggered Marlin's demise, there was little for him to do but soldier around, knowing his chance for victory was gone.

With Marlin gone, the race looked like Allison's to win.

Davey built a 1.34-second lead, but with just over 30 laps remaining in the race, a piece of debris on the track brought out the final yellow, and gave Wallace the chance he needed. With a four-tire pit stop of 17.1 seconds, Wallace's crew beat Davey's on pit road, and the Miller Pontiac emerged in the lead as the cars lined up for restart.

While Rusty pulled away to a 1.31-second victory at the front, Davey became embroiled in a war with Martin. Martin won the battle, and Davey finished third, ahead of Dale Jarrett.

Rudd finished fifth, with Marlin taking sixth and Gordon emerging as the final car on the lead lap.

Earnhardt ended up losing four laps during the course of the day and was classified 26th — to the delight of Jarrett and Wallace. Wallace gained 95 points in the point chase, while Jarrett gained 80 to chop the margin to 181 after the 16th event of the season. Wallace climbed to third in the point standings with his victory, but he still trailed by 260.

Morgan Shepherd was fourth in the point standings, with Allison moving up to fifth in the standings.

Kyle Petty, Gordon, Martin, Schrader and Irvan completed the top-10 in points at the conclusion of the Slick 50 300.

The entire field of drivers salutes the crowd at New Hampshire International Speedway.

Dick Bahre's New Hampshire International Speedway had a full house for its first NASCAR Winston Cup event.

Fin. Pos.	Str. Pos.	Driver	Team	Fin. Pos.	Str. Pos.	Driver	Team
1	33	Rusty Wallace	Miller Genuine Draft Pontiac	21	25	Kenny Wallace	Dirt Devil Pontiac
2	1	Mark Martin	Valvoline Ford	22	38	Derrike Cope	Bojangles' Ford
3	7	Davey Allison	Havoline Ford	23	12	Michael Waltrip	Pennzoil Pontiac
4	9	Dale Jarrett	Interstate Batteries Chevrolet	24	20	Ted Musgrave	Jasper Engines Ford
5	10	Ricky Rudd	Tide Chevrolet	25	32	Hut Stricklin	McDonald's Ford
6	2	Sterling Marlin	Raybestos Ford	26	24	Dale Earnhardt	GM Goodwrench Chevrolet
7	3	Jeff Gordon	DuPont Auto Finishes Chevrolet	27	31	Wally Dallenbach	Keystone Beer Ford
8	19	Kyle Petty	Mello Yello Pontiac	28	16	Rick Wilson	STP Pontiac
9	18	Bill Elliott	Budweiser Ford	29	35	Ken Bouchard	Burger King Ford
10	17	Bobby Labonte	Maxwell House Ford	30	34	Dave Marcis	AEL Rentals Chevrolet
11	13	Jimmy Hensley	Purolator Ford	31	5	Terry Labonte	Kellogg's Chevrolet
12	27	Geoff Bodine	Motorcraft Ford	32	30	Greg Sacks	Country Time Ford
13	23	Brett Bodine	Quaker State Ford	33	37	Dick Trickle	Factory Stores Ford
14	14	Morgan Shepherd	Citgo Ford	34	40	Jimmy Means	Hurley Limo Ford
15	8	Ernie Irvan	Kodak Film Chevrolet	35	21	Lake Speed	Purex Ford
16	26	Rick Mast	Skoal Classic Ford	36	15	Joe Nemechek	Dentyne Chevrolet
17	29	Harry Gant	Skoal Bandit Chevrolet	37	6	Jeff Burton	TIC Financial Ford
18	11	Jimmy Spencer	Meineke Mufflers Ford	38	4	Ken Schrader	Kodiak Chevrolet
19	22	Darrell Waltrip	Western Auto Chevrolet	39	39	Phil Parsons	Manheim Auctions Chevrolet
20	28	Bobby Hillin	Heilig-Meyers Ford	40	36	Jerry O'Neil	Aroneck Racing Chevrolet

MILLER GENUINE DRAFT 500

*I*t was a scene of grand simplicity. A moment frozen in time that made the hair on one's arms stand on end, with chills creeping up the back. A gesture so pure, so genuine, so sensitive that it made one blink back tears and swallow mightily.

It was merely a group of black-clad men, kneeling with arms around each other's shoulders. That it came on the start/finish line was unique. That it took the place of a winning team's usual jubilant high-fives and Gatorade-dumping was the most touching part of all.

Jack-man David Smith led the team in prayer. And tens of thousands of fans stood and watched in approving silence while it took place.

Kenny Schrader and Bill Elliott led the field from their front-row starting positions. Elliott finished third and Schrader sixth in the 200-lapper.

After his victory at Pocono, Dale Earhardt hoists a flag bearing the number 28, in honor of Davey Allison.

RICHARD PETTY "200" VICTORY CIRCLE

NASCAR Winston Cup Series

POCONO U.S.A.

ne Draft

e Draft

When it was over, the black car made its backwards victory lap, with the winning driver holding a flag out the window, a lap of honor for two friends and a tribute to the accomplishments of fellow competitors.

The entire activity lasted just a minute or two. But in that short span of time, it showed just how deeply the NASCAR Winston Cup family cares when part of it is lost.

Davey Allison left New Hampshire a week earlier with a song in his heart. He had battled throughout the day for the victory and finished third, behind Rusty and Mark Martin. When he left New Hampshire, he had climbed to fifth in the standings and he felt his team was in the midst of putting it all together. "His" tracks were coming

took the 30-minute trip to the world's biggest superspeedway to see Neil Bonnett's son test his Busch Grand National car in preparation for that race at Talladega.

Inexplicably, the helicopter crashed while landing and Davey was severely injured in the wreck. He was taken by medical helicopter to Birmingham where, 18 hours later, he died.

Davey's death dealt a body-blow to the Winston Cup family, already reeling from the shock of losing its defending champion just over two months earlier. Hearts were wrenched for Bobby

Immediately after his victory, Dale Earnhardt's crew knelt around his car to remember Davey Allison.

up, and he felt that, with a little luck, he could be in the hunt for the championship when it came to the stretch run for the title.

Monday afternoon after the New Hampshire race, he flew his recently-purchased helicopter to Talladega from his new home in Hueytown. Long-time friend Red Farmer was on board as the two

and Judy Allison.

When the competitors assembled at Dr. Joe Mattioli's triangular superspeedway, practice and qualifying were the order of the day—but few had their hearts in it. And that included Joe and his wife Rose, who had become close friends with the Allisons over the years. It was ironic that just five

The field heads into action through the flat third turn at Pocono.

weeks ago, they had presented the Allison family with Pocono's Bill France Award for outstanding contributions to the sport.

When qualifying was completed, Kenny Schrader had put another new lap record on the books, but the normally witty Schrader was subdued as well. Alan's death had been tough—but dealing with Davey's was even more difficult than many could imagine.

Bill Elliott had one of his better qualifying runs of the season, and would start outside Kenny on the front row. Ricky Rudd and Ernie Irvan made up the second row, with Mark Martin and Jimmy Hensley right behind them. Bobby Labonte had an outstanding run to qualify seventh, alongside Morgan Shepherd, while Derrike Cope and Brett Bodine filled out the top-ten.

Dale Earnhardt qualified 11th, Rusty Wallace 18th and Dale Jarrett 23rd.

From the start, this race at Pocono looked like it could be anyone's victory. Within the first 75

laps, nine different drivers had exchanged the lead, with Earnhardt hovering around the top five like a mother hen.

Dale Jarrett and Kyle Petty looked strong enough to win, but Kyle tore the clutch out of his Mello Yello Pontiac when he exited the pit road on lap 129. His hopes had ended. Jarrett's chances faded when he came in on a yellow flag to top off fuel and lost track position.

The race came down to a battle between Wallace and Earnhardt again, and Earnhardt moved to the lead for the final laps left in the race, driving under Wallace in the first turn, out-racing the Pontiac to the flatter tunnel turn, and then keeping Rusty at bay to win by just over three-quarters of a second.

Elliott brought his Budweiser Ford home in third place, his best finish of the season, while Shepherd was fourth in the Wood Brothers' Citgo Ford. Brett Bodine finally shook the "can't finish" label and brought the Quaker State Ford to fifth place, just ahead of pole-sitter Schrader.

In all, there were 15 drivers on the lead lap at the conclusion of the 200-lapper, with Sterling Marlin, Jarrett, Harry Gant and Darrell Waltrip filling out the top-ten.

When the checkered flag fell, Earnhardt continued on his cool-down lap. He stopped at the start/finish line and his team ran to the Goodwrench Chevrolet. Car-owner Richard Childress handed Dale the "28" flag and the team knelt in prayer for Davey, his wife Liz and their children, as well as for Alan. Kyle, in hopes of winning, had carried the flag inside his car until he saw his chances for victory were gone. He then sent the flag down pit road to be given to the race winner to carry aloft during the Kulwicki Victory Lap.

After the lap, Earnhardt pulled into victory lane. It took Dale a couple of minutes to pull himself together. Fans used to the gruff "Intimidator" had a chance to see beneath the game face Dale wears at the race track. They saw, instead, the person who really IS Dale Earnhardt. They saw a sensitive man who has been deeply touched by the loss of two of the brightest lights in the future of the sport. Dale had fished and hunted with one. The other he respected greatly after he defeated all odds to fulfill his greatest dream of a championship.

The Intimidator blinked back his own tears and gathered himself together. He had increased his point lead and had notched his fifth victory of the season.

Kenny Schrader's pole position was his fourth of the season.

Dale Earnhardt flashes to his fifth win of the year in front of a huge throng at Pocono.

Fin. Pos.	Str. Pos.	Driver	Team	Fin. Pos.	Str. Pos.	Driver	Team
1	11	Dale Earnhardt	GM Goodwrench Chevrolet	21	25	Rick Wilson	STP Pontiac
2	18	Rusty Wallace	Miller Genuine Draft Pontiac	22	36	Dave Marcis	York Springs Auto Auction Chevrolet
3	2	Bill Elliott	Budweiser Ford	23	30	Kenny Wallace	Dirt Devil Pontiac
4	8	Morgan Shepherd	Citgo Ford	24	24	Jimmy Spencer	Meineke Mufflers Ford
5	10	Brett Bodine	Quaker State Ford	25	37	Ken Bouchard	Burger King Ford
6	1	Ken Schrader	Kodiak Chevrolet	26	35	Jimmy Horton	Active Trucking Chevrolet
7	15	Sterling Marlin	Raybestos Ford	27	19	Kyle Petty	Mello Yello Pontiac
8	23	Dale Jarrett	Interstate Batteries Chevrolet	28	12	Hut Stricklin	McDonald's Ford
9	21	Harry Gant	Skoal Bandit Chevrolet	29	9	Derrike Cope	Bojangles' Ford
10	27	Darrell Waltrip	Western Auto Chevrolet	30	31	Dick Trickle	Factory Stores Ford
11	3	Ricky Rudd	Tide Chevrolet	31	4	Ernie Irvan	Kodak Film Chevrolet
12	13	Geoff Bodine	Motorcraft Ford	32	26	Greg Sacks	Country Time Ford
13	5	Mark Martin	Valvoline Ford	33	17	Ted Musgrave	Jasper Engines Ford
14	16	Michael Waltrip	Pennzoil Pontiac	34	38	Kerry Teague	Linro Chevrolet
15	7	Bobby Labonte	Maxwell House Ford	35	40	John Krebs	Diamond Ridge Chevrolet
16	32	Terry Labonte	Kellogg's Chevrolet	36	29	Rick Mast	Skoal Classic Ford
17	22	Wally Dallenbach	Keystone Beer Ford	37	20	Jeff Gordon	DuPont Auto Finishes Chevrolet
18	28	Phil Parsons	Manheim Auctions Chevrolet	38	39	Clay Young	Belden Asphalt Ford
19	34	Bobby Hamilton	Holgate Toy Company Ford	39	6	Jimmy Hensley	Purolator Ford
20	14	Bobby Hillin	Heilig-Meyers Ford	40	33	T.W. Taylor	Children's Miracle Network Ford

DIEHARD 500

The emotional shot taken by the NASCAR Winston Cup family in the week prior to the Pocono race carried over to Talladega. It was, after all, Davey Allison's "home" track, and the Robert Yates Racing Ford was back in a garage stall, with Robbie Gordon behind the wheel.

As the teams prepared for qualifying, Dale Earnhardt knew he had slightly shaken loose from his pursuers. He wasn't home free, by any means, but his win at Pocono had shown his team was capable of bouncing back after the New Hampshire debacle.

Earnhardt's point lead was 209 over fellow Chevrolet driver Dale Jarrett, and Rusty Wallace was now 260 markers behind the Goodwrench Chevrolet. Morgan Shepherd was fourth in the standings, with Kenny Schrader fifth, but neither had proven to be able to race week-to-week with the point leaders.

The race for the championship appeared to be narrowing down to the top three, unless all had problems and someone else got very hot, indeed.

Robby Gordon raced well in Robert Yates' Ford, but later wrecked. Here, he battles with Rick Wilson.

After winning the pole, Bill Elliott's day ended with an 11th place finish.

Bill Elliott had suffered through one of the most disappointing seasons of his career. His third-place finish the previous week at Pocono had been his first top-five of the year—unbelievable as it seemed. He had qualified second-fastest at Pocono, his best start since the Goodwrench 500 at Rockingham in February.

Headed into the Talladega fray, he was 15th in the point standings, more than 650 points out of the title chase, and Elliott knew he would have to battle to pick up the 150 points that separated him from a place in the top-10.

The betting for the pole was on either Earnhardt, who had been blistering at Daytona and Talladega, Ernie Irvan, who had won three of the last five restrictor-plate races and Kyle Petty, the Daytona 500 pole-sitter.

Elliott was somewhat overlooked, but he had been fast at Daytona in both races.

The "big guns" took turns knocking each other out of the top qualifying position, and finally, with just two cars remaining in line behind him, Elliott headed for the lap that would give him his first pole since May 1992 at Charlotte.

Irvan ended up second, alongside Elliott, while Brett Bodine continued his strong qualifying efforts with a third-fastest lap. It was Brett's seventh top-four performance of the season. Outside Brett was Kyle Petty, with Ricky Rudd and Rick Mast making up the third row.

Greg Sacks was a sparkling seventh-fastest,

with Jeff Gordon alongside him. Hut Stricklin and Rick Wilson made up the fifth row, with Earnhardt 11th-fastest. Dale Jarrett was 15th-quick, while Rusty Wallace struggled, and would start from the 32nd position.

And Neil Bonnett, making his first start since 1990, took his Richard Childress-owned Chevrolet to 20th in the starting order, a solid position for the driver who said he just wanted "to stay around on the lead lap, shake the rust off and have a chance at the end for a good finish."

Before Sunday's race began, Terry Labonte was nominated to fill in for Davey Allison in the remaining Dodge IROC race of the season at Michigan. Davey was leading the Dodge IROC point standings, and it was announced that Davey's earnings from the series would go to a trust fund for his children.

Harry Hyde joined the Harry Melling team

as team manager for P.J. Jones and Wally Dallenbach asked for and received his release from Jack Roush to seek a different ride for the 1994 season. At the same time, Ted Musgrave started narrowing down his choices for 1994, leaving the RaDiUs Ford open for another driver next year.

As a tribute to Davey, Donnie Allison took the Texaco show car on a lap around Talladega in pre-race activities and Liz Allison addressed the huge throng, expressing the family's thanks to the fans for their outpouring of sentiment during the previous two weeks.

Finally, it was time for the crapshoot to begin. Talladega has always been the site of exciting racing, and this Sunday would be no different.

The packs of cars formed early, and Ernie Irvan quickly proved he was capable of winning yet another restrictor-plate race, pulling past Elliott after the first lap. Kyle, Earnhardt and Elliott, along with Rudd, all battled for the lead early, swapping it back and forth.

Jarrett, Martin and Gordon joined the list of leaders, but Earnhardt had proven he could go to the front whenever he wanted.

The race had its dramas. Gordon, running in fifth place, got too low on Talladega's apron while trying to go three-wide on lap 56 and slid up the track, hitting the wall and ending his day.

Just 14 laps later, a six-car wreck involved Jimmy Horton, Ritchie Petty, Rick Mast, Stanley Smith, Kenny Wallace and Loy Allen, Jr..

On lap 132, Bonnett had an accident in the Childress car that also ended Musgrave's hopes

Bill Elliott notched his first pole position of the season, but was only able to post an 11th-place finish in his Budweiser Ford.

Ernie Irvan and Ricky Rudd hustle off pit road. Irvan would battle Earnhardt for the victory and settle for second place.

for his first career victory.

The race restarted with 40 laps to go—and 25 cars on the lead lap. If everyone held together for the final 100 miles, it promised to be a dogfight.

But one by one, some of the contenders fell away. Elliott was squeezed into the wall and knocked the toe-in out of the Budweiser Ford.

Finally, with just four laps to go, Earnhardt moved to the inside and past Kyle for the lead. Irvan and Jarrett helped push Dale through, and within a matter of seconds, Kyle was fourth.

With everyone behind him starting to race for position, Earnhardt pulled out a brief lead, but Irvan narrowed it on the final lap. Coming off the last turn and heading for the flag, Earnhardt and Irvan were alongside each other and Dale moved over to get a draft off the side of Irvan. That move boosted his black Chevrolet to the front of the yellow Lumina—and it was enough to give Earnhardt a six-inch victory in one of the tightest finishes in NASCAR history.

Martin finished third, with Petty fourth. Jarrett came home fifth in the mad scramble, ahead of Sacks and Shepherd.

The win was the 59th of Earnhardt's career and, combined with Jarrett's fifth place and Wallace's 17th, increased his point lead.

As the teams headed for Watkins Glen, Earnhardt was now 234 points ahead of Jarrett—and 333 points ahead of Wallace. Shepherd was fourth in the points, and Martin had climbed into fifth place.

The Earnhardt victory boosted Chevrolet into a 21-point lead over Pontiac in the Manufacturer's Championship. The Bowtie Brigade had nine wins and 129 points after the first 18 races, while Pontiac had six wins and 108 points. Defending champion Ford was in third place with a mere three victories—and 105 points.

The final road race of the season was next, and the teams headed home for a few days before moving up the east coast to upstate New York.

Donnie Allison salutes the crowd while driving Davey's car in a parade lap prior to the start of the DieHard 500.

Fin. Pos.	Str. Pos.	Driver	Team	Fin. Pos.	Str. Pos.	Driver	Team
1	11	Dale Earnhardt	GM Goodwrench Chevrolet	22	37	Phil Parsons	Manheim Auctions Chevrolet
2	2	Ernie Irvan	Kodak Film Chevrolet	23	10	Rick Wilson	STP Pontiac
3	25	Mark Martin	Valvoline Ford	24	5	Ricky Rudd	Tide Chevrolet
4	4	Kyle Petty	Mello Yello Pontiac	25	17	Jimmy Means	NAPA Ford
5	15	Dale Jarrett	Interstate Batteries Chevrolet	26	18	Loy Allen	Naturally Fresh Ford
6	7	Greg Sacks	Country Time Ford	27	22	Sterling Marlin	Raybestos Ford
7	23	Morgan Shepherd	Citgo Ford	28	19	Jimmy Hensley	Family Channel Ford
8	12	Harry Gant	Skoal Bandit Chevrolet	29	42	Dave Marcis	STG Chevrolet
9	3	Brett Bodine	Quaker State Ford	30	27	Jimmy Spencer	Meineke Mufflers Ford
10	26	Wally Dallenbach	Keystone Beer Ford	31	8	Jeff Gordon	DuPont Auto Finishes Chevrolet
11	1	Bill Elliott	Budweiser Ford	32	28	Ken Schrader	Kodiak Chevrolet
12	9	Hut Stricklin	McDonald's Ford	33	21	Ted Musgrave	Jasper Engines Ford
13	29	Bobby Hillin	Heilig-Meyers Ford	34	20	Neil Bonnett	Mom 'n' Pops Chevrolet
14	36	Terry Labonte	Kellogg's Chevrolet	35	34	Kenny Wallace	Dirt Devil Pontiac
15	41	Bobby Labonte	Maxwell House Ford	36	31	Derrike Cope	Bojangles' Ford
16	33	Geoff Bodine	Motorcraft Ford	37	16	Darrell Waltrip	Western Auto Chevrolet
17	32	Rusty Wallace	Miller Genuine Draft Pontiac	38	6	Rick Mast	Skoal Classic Ford
18	40	Lake Speed	Purex Ford	39	24	Jimmy Horton	Active Trucking Chevrolet
19	38	Dick Trickle	Factory Stores Ford	40	35	Stanley Smith	BS&S Motorsports Chevrolet
20	13	Michael Waltrip	Pennzoil Pontiac	41	39	Ritchie Petty	Le Bleu Ford
21	30	Jeff Purvis	Phoenix Construction Chevrolet	42	14	Robby Gordon	Havoline Ford

BUD AT THE GLEN

Mark Martin's Valvoline Ford was a blur throughout the Watkins weekend. His victory was well-deserved.

With "Race Fever" taking over upstate New York as it does only at the Watkins Glen race, there were plenty of autograph sessions, breakfasts and luncheons with area civic leaders and golf tournaments to make the days preceding the Budweiser at The Glen flash past.

The only thing that would make the event at The Glen more spectacular would be to have it in late September or early October, when the hardwood forests and miles of vineyards take on their fall coloring.

With the setting for the event in some of the most beautiful countryside America has to offer, there were also plenty of changes as the transporters unloaded their cargoes for the battle around the 2.43-mile road course located on a hillside overlooking Seneca Lake.

Todd Bodine, expected to make the jump to NASCAR Winston Cup racing for the 1994 season, showed up a little early. Prior to The Glen's event, he was

Rusty Wallace battled throughout the day at Watkins Glen, but had to settle for a l9th-place finish.

Dale Earnhardt takes his Goodwrench Chevrolet through its paces before colliding with a spinning Kyle Petty.

named to drive the RahMoc Racing Thunderbird for the remainder of the season and on into 1994.

Dick Trickle, who had driven the RahMoc Factory Outlet Stores Fords throughout the year, was looking for another ride.

Robert Yates Racing had Lake Speed behind the wheel of the Havoline Ford, where he would remain for the "foreseeable future" while Yates and company made the decision of who would be the replacement driver for Davey Allison for the 1994 season.

In the weekend prior to The Glen, Terry Labonte had taken his substitute driving role in the Dodge IROC Series very seriously. He had filled in for Davey in the final race of the year at Michigan, and did nothing less than finish exactly where he had to—sixth—to clinch the series championship for Davey. The $175,000 prize money went into a trust fund for Davey's children. Ironically, it was the first—and only—championship on which Davey would ever have his name. He had never won one before—at a track or in a series.

Michael Kranefuss, the worldwide head of Ford's racing programs, and the man most responsible for returning Ford to a position of leadership in the NASCAR world, announced his retirement as of November 1.

No, that wasn't all. Kellogg's decided to follow Terry Labonte to Hendrick Motorsport for next season, leaving Billy Hagan searching for both a driver and a sponsor.

And there were a couple of "semi-new" faces in the Glen garage as Tommy Kendall returned for another outing in the Kulwicki Racing Ford and Dorsey Schroeder slid through the window of the Tri-Star Motorsports Country Time Lemonade Ford.

It had, indeed, been a busy 10 days since Talladega!

After all the hoopla, it was time for qualifying, and when the session was over, Mark Martin had smoked 'em.

There was nothing to do but shake heads in awe. Martin had turned the most perfect lap since the Winston Cup cars had come to Watkins Glen in 1986. The lap was merely 2.5 miles per hour faster than the previous lap record—and well over a mile an hour faster than second-place Kenny Schrader's super-quick lap.

Martin could only say that he hit everything right in the corners, had a fast car and tried to get it back to the start/finish line without going off course. Whatever he did, he did it right!

Speed, the first time he sat behind the wheel of the 28, put the Havoline Ford fourth on the grid, with Terry Labonte inside him after the Texan turned the third-fastest lap.

Dale Earnhardt continued his strong road course qualifying performances with a fifth-fastest lap, while Rusty Wallace, desperate for points to close the gap on Earnhardt, qualified sixth.

Kyle Petty and Bill Elliott made up the fourth row, with Ricky Rudd and Wally Dallenbach, still searching for his first Winston Cup victory, completing the top-ten.

Ernie Irvan, hoping to do well in front of thousands of Kodak employees from nearby Rochester, qualified his Chevrolet 12th-fastest and would start alongside Jeff Gordon.

There was no question that Mark had the fastest car in the field when it came time for the green flag to drop in front of the huge throng packed into the track. Some wags wondered if he could, indeed, lap the field on his way to his first victory of the season.

Others, noting the problems that had befallen Mark throughout the season when it appeared he had the fastest car, wondered what would be the cause of a loss for the Valvoline team this time.

Martin left no doubt from the start that if he had a trouble-free run, he would be the one to beat. Time after time during the first half of the race Martin blasted past those in front of him on restarts, took his accustomed place at the point—and drove away to a lead.

Then, what appeared to be disaster struck the Jack Roush-owned team once again. During the fourth caution flag, a lug nut rounded off and Martin had fallen from first to 25th by the time the team could solve the problem and change his tires.

The flat first turn at Watkins Glen is always an action spot in Winston Cup events at the road course.

From then on, Martin only became more determined. He began slashing his way through the field, but with only 35 laps to go, didn't know if he had enough time to get all the way to the front once again.

Three caution flags helped him, and few paid his charge mind as Earnhardt and Wallace and Petty went at it hammer and tongs at the front of the pack.

With nine laps to go, the final yellow waved when Waltrip smacked the tire barrier in the final turn, and Martin was able to close the gap on the leaders.

Only seven laps remained when the green

Lake Speed took over the Robert Yates Ford at The Glen and qualified fourth.

Mark Martin's victory came from the pole, and he cashed Unocal's big check.

He finished a position behind Earnhardt, but never led a lap, and lost another eight points to Dale in the point race.

Rookies Bobby Labonte, P.J. Jones and Kenny Wallace all had excellent finishes, coming home seventh, eighth and ninth. Schroeder was out early after a first-lap wreck, Dale Jarrett lost his clutch and finished 32nd and Lake Speed was classified

flew with Martin in ninth position on the restart. Within one lap he was fifth, and after that he was third, behind Kyle and Earnhardt.

Whether Mark could have gotten the two became a moot point when Kyle lost it heading into the Esses, spun, and collected Earnhardt.

Martin drove into the smoke—and emerged on the other side in the lead. Nothing would keep him from the victory this day.

He cruised home to a 3.84-second victory over teammate Dallenbach, giving Roush Racing its first NASCAR Winston Cup one-two.

Jimmy Spencer survived all day and finished third, and Bill Elliott brought the Budweiser Ford home fourth. Schrader was fifth, with Sterling Marlin sixth.

In all, 19 cars finished on the lead lap, with Wallace the final car on the lead lap after losing a cylinder in the waning laps of the race.

Daddy Darrell and "Unkie Mike" share a light moment with Darrell's daughter, Jessica.

27th after running in the top five before spinning in the last turn of the road course.

The enjoyable week at The Glen was over. Michigan was next on the schedule, the final event of the year at a speedway more than 1.5 miles in length.

JIM RIESBECK ··································

*H*e was a local boy who made good, rising from a clerk in one of the Corning Glass Works plants to controller and executive vice-president of Corning, Inc. He collected Corvettes and made excursions with friends on his Harley.

He saw his first stock car race at Daytona in February, 1983. Three months later, he convinced Corning, Inc.'s Board of Directors that the bankrupt Watkins Glen road racing course should be purchased to mainline a life-giving injection into the local tourist economy. The board agreed, Corning bought The Glen — and changed its name to Watkins Glen International.

Jim Riesbeck became the chairman and chief executive officer of WGI, and just three years after he saw his first NASCAR Winston Cup race, The Glen became the site of the Bud at The Glen.

More than 125,000 fans flocked to the 2.4-mile circuit this year to see the eighth running of the Bud at The Glen.

Sadly, Jim wasn't there to greet them. Six weeks prior to the running of the race, he died of heart failure at the age of 50.

In eight short years, he had a profound impact on the quality of life in the Finger Lakes Region. He was the person most instrumental in returning The Glen to its place at the pinnacle of road racing in this country, and he did it in his own folksy way. He may have been an executive, but he was just "Jim" to everyone who knew him.

He was a person who cared for his fellow man and took his responsibilities seriously. He served on the boards of the Corning Community College foundation, the local chapter of the American Red Cross and Guthrie Health Care Systems.

His wife, Joyce, his mother, Isadora and his son, Bryan, will miss him.

So will we.

Fin. Pos.	Str. Pos.	Driver	Team	Fin. Pos.	Str. Pos.	Driver	Team
1	1	Mark Martin	Valvoline Ford	20	27	Brett Bodine	Quaker State Ford
2	10	Wally Dallenbach	Keystone Beer Ford	21	13	Joe Nemechek	Cintas Chevrolet
3	32	Jimmy Spencer	Meineke Mufflers Ford	22	23	Rick Wilson	STP Pontiac
4	8	Bill Elliott	Budweiser Ford	23	3	Terry Labonte	Kellogg's Chevrolet
5	2	Ken Schrader	Kodiak Chevrolet	24	9	Ricky Rudd	Tide Chevrolet
6	30	Sterling Marlin	Raybestos Ford	25	33	Tommy Kendall	Family Channel Ford
7	24	Bobby Labonte	Maxwell House Ford	26	7	Kyle Petty	Mello Yello Pontiac
8	29	P.J. Jones	Tops Friendly Markets Ford	27	4	Lake Speed	Havoline Ford
9	19	Kenny Wallace	Dirt Devil Pontiac	28	22	Morgan Shepherd	Citgo Ford
10	18	Harry Gant	Skoal Bandit Chevrolet	29	38	Scott Gaylord	Oliver Manufacturing Oldsmobile
11	15	Derrike Cope	Bojangles' Ford	30	34	Todd Bodine	Factory Stores Ford
12	26	Michael Waltrip	Pennzoil Pontiac	31	11	Jeff Gordon	DuPont Auto Finishes Chevrolet
13	28	Scott Lagasse	Pedigree Food Chevrolet	32	14	Dale Jarrett	Interstate Batteries Chevrolet
14	25	Darrell Waltrip	Western Auto Chevrolet	33	20	Phil Parsons	Manheim Auctions Chevrolet
15	12	Ernie Irvan	Kodak Film Chevrolet	34	36	Ted Musgrave	Jasper Engines Ford
16	16	Geoff Bodine	Motorcraft Ford	35	17	Bobby Hillin	Heilig-Meyers Ford
17	37	Hut Stricklin	McDonald's Ford	36	35	Ed Ferree	Frankland Racing Chevrolet
18	5	Dale Earnhardt	GM Goodwrench Chevrolet	37	31	Rick Mast	Skoal Classic Ford
19	6	Rusty Wallace	Miller Genuine Draft Pontiac	38	21	Dorsey Schroeder	Country Time Ford

CHAMPION SPARK PLUG 400

When the teams left Michigan after the June outing on Roger Penske's two-mile oval, Ricky Rudd had claimed the victory by shrewdly playing the gas-mileage game.

Now, just two months later, the teams returned for what has become one of the most important races of the season. The points don't count any more than they do for a North Wilkesboro or a Phoenix victory, but the August Champion Spark Plug 400 is the last race of the year in Michigan. It's the one the executives of Ford, Chevrolet and Pontiac remember most during the cold Detroit winter.

Some wags say that Detroit winters last from September 1 until July 4—and the sun

Suites on the inside of pit road offer great viewing spots for the crowd at Michigan.

Mark Martin gave owner Jack Roush a "hometown" victory at Michigan. Roush's business is located in nearby Livonia.

In front of another sell-out, Ricky Rudd was unable to duplicate his June victory at Michigan.

shines no more than three days during that stretch. If that's the case, then pleasant memories of the August Michigan race are a must during the dreary, gray Michigan winter.

So, everyone brings their best to Michigan—and all the stops are pulled out for a victory the second time around in the Irish Hills.

Dale Earnhardt had punched his point lead up to 281 over Dale Jarrett and 343 over Rusty Wallace. It was easy to understand Earnhardt's smiling countenance. He looked like he was well on his way to his sixth Winston Cup title—an accomplishment few thought any driver could obtain in the ultra-competitive world of NASCAR Winston Cup racing.

Mark Martin had climbed to fourth in the point standings, just 25 points ahead of Morgan Shepherd, who had continued to assemble a superb season with the Wood Brothers Fords. In 19 races, Morgan had 11 top-10 finishes.

Kyle Petty headed for Michigan in sixth place in the standings, still smarting from the mistake that cost him a chance to win at Watkins Glen the

weekend before. He was only 27 points ahead of Kenny Schrader, with Ernie Irvan, Geoff Bodine and rookie Jeff Gordon occupying the remaining top-10 positions in the point standings.

Jack Roush's engineering business is located in nearby Livonia, a Detroit suburb, and Jack always makes sure his teams prepare well for the Michigan race. It's important to him from a Ford standpoint, but also for the morale of his company employees, many of whom have their only opportunity of the year to see the Roush Racing cars perform.

At Michigan, Roush announced that Ted Musgrave would become the driver of his second team car, beginning with the 1994 season.

Roush's sky-high team rolled into Michigan with vengeance in their eyes. They had won the week before, taking advantage of the Kyle Petty/Dale Earnhardt mishap, but no one questioned the victory. Mark had been the fastest car at the track all week.

But not one team member

Kenny Schrader won his fifth pole of the season and Lake Speed had the second-fastest lap to lead the field away for the Champion Spark Plug 400 at MIS.

had forgotten the June Michigan race. They felt the track owed them a victory, particularly after Mark had led nearly three-quarters of the Miller 400 before being aced out by Rudd's fuel mileage antics.

Long hours had been spent preparing the Valvoline Ford for the Michigan race. The team went about its work grimly, determined to take home the trophy.

Goodyear had brought a new radial tire for the Michigan race, and when qualifying was over, it was obvious that the company had done its homework in providing a fast, but safe, tire for competition.

No less than 12 drivers, led by Kenny Schrader, broke the old track record, with Schrader's pole lap well over 2.5 miles per hour faster than the mark set last August by Alan Kulwicki. It took everything Schrader had in his Kodiak Chevrolet to snatch the pole from Lake Speed in the Havoline Ford.

Rudd showed he hadn't lost his liking for MIS,

posting the third-fastest lap, just ahead of Shepherd. Musgrave celebrated his new deal with Roush by qualifying fifth in the RaDiUs Ford—his best starting position since a fifth in the second race of the year at Rockingham.

Todd Bodine, in only his second race with the Factory Outlet Stores Ford, was right beside Musgrave, while Dale Earnhardt and Bill Elliott made up the fourth row for Sunday's 200-lapper.

Rookie Jeff Gordon continued his impressive showing, starting ninth, alongside Rusty Wallace. Bobby Labonte lined up right behind fellow yellow-striper Gordon, with Martin notching the 12th-fastest lap.

Dale Jarrett continued to have qualifying problems, and would start 27th. Ernie Irvan, who had flown home to Charlotte to welcome his daughter into the world, returned with an ear-to-ear grin, but would start 24th.

For the first half of the race, it appeared that Rudd might be the driver to sweep both Michigan races. And it quickly became apparent that the

Jeff Gordon had another outstanding run at Michigan, finishing third after leading late in the race.

crowd were locked on the three-way battle for fifth, with the photo-finish camera at the start/finish line used to determine the finishing positions of Musgrave, Wallace and Speed. Musgrave's dive to the inside took fifth, with Wallace just nipping Speed for sixth.

Where was the series point-leader?

Earnhardt cut a tire with 40 laps remaining, and lost a lap while his crew made the tire change. Dale managed to get back on the lead lap when he beat Gordon to the line when the next-to-last caution flag came out, and finished ninth, just ahead of Elliott. In all, there were 15 cars on the lead lap at the end of the race.

Bobby Labonte continued to impress in his rookie season. He notched his second-straight top-10 finish by grabbing eighth place.

Jarrett's fourth enabled him to gain 22 points on Earnhardt and he now trailed the leader by

hard work by Martin's team had paid off. Mark was the only driver who looked like he could tough it out and run with Rudd.

But just after the halfway point, the Tide Chevrolet developed engine problems, and Ricky's hopes for a sweep were over. And as soon as Rudd had his problems, the race belonged to Martin.

He had to battle a little, here and there, particularly when he came out off pit road slightly in arrears during caution periods.

But he could move to the front and once there, pull away from the field. He led 81 of the last 100 laps, and eased to a 1.28-second victory over Shepherd.

The victory was one he savored, because he had won the Busch Grand National race in dominant fashion the day before—and the Sunday win allowed him to accomplish a goal he had set some time ago—to win on Saturday and Sunday during the same weekend at the same track.

Gordon, who had led earlier in the race, finished third in another outstanding performance in the DuPont Chevrolet. He wasn't a threat at the end, but ran a heady race throughout the 400 miles.

Jarrett hammered his way through the field to a fourth-place finish, but the eyes of the sold-out

Ricky Rudd's team did their best on pit road, but Mark Martin was just too strong at Michigan.

259. Wallace gained 17 points.

The Blue Oval boys would have the bragging rights for the long Michigan winter, thanks to Martin, Roush and the hard-working crew.

And as the fans filed out of the grandstands, the crews loaded their charges. The long run home to the shops would be delayed by a couple of days.

The much-anticipated test session at Indianapolis Motor Speedway was next on the agenda, and drivers, crew members and car owners couldn't wait to head down the highway for what would be, for many, a chance they never thought they would have.

The opportunity to put laps on The Brickyard.

Mark Martin and wife Arlene treat son Matthew to a victory lane at Michigan.

Fin. Pos.	Str. Pos.	Driver	Team	Fin. Pos.	Str. Pos.	Driver	Team
1	12	Mark Martin	Valvoline Ford	22	38	Dave Marcis	STG Chevrolet
2	4	Morgan Shepherd	Citgo Ford	23	14	Kenny Wallace	Dirt Devil Pontiac
3	9	Jeff Gordon	DuPont Auto Finishes Chevrolet	24	26	Geoff Bodine	Motorcraft Ford
4	27	Dale Jarrett	Interstate Batteries Chevrolet	25	31	Jimmy Means	Hurley Limo Ford
5	5	Ted Musgrave	Jasper Engines Ford	26	39	P.J. Jones	Melling Racing Ford
6	10	Rusty Wallace	Miller Genuine Draft Pontiac	27	1	Ken Schrader	Kodiak Chevrolet
7	2	Lake Speed	Havoline Ford	28	29	Rick Wilson	STP Pontiac
8	11	Bobby Labonte	Maxwell House Ford	29	41	Terry Labonte	Kellogg's Chevrolet
9	7	Dale Earnhardt	GM Goodwrench Chevrolet	30	20	Harry Gant	Skoal Bandit Chevrolet
10	8	Bill Elliott	Budweiser Ford	31	35	Wally Dallenbach	Keystone Beer Ford
11	18	Bobby Hillin	Heilig-Meyers Ford	32	24	Ernie Irvan	Kodak Film Chevrolet
12	13	Greg Sacks	Country Time Ford	33	16	Rick Mast	Skoal Classic Ford
13	30	Darrell Waltrip	Western Auto Chevrolet	34	37	Hut Stricklin	McDonald's Ford
14	19	Brett Bodine	Quaker State Ford	35	3	Ricky Rudd	Tide Chevrolet
15	15	Jimmy Hensley	USA Bobsled Ford	36	33	Jim Sauter	Evinrude Ford
16	28	Michael Waltrip	Pennzoil Pontiac	37	21	Joe Nemechek	Cintas Chevrolet
17	34	Sterling Marlin	Raybestos Ford	38	23	Jimmy Horton	Active Trucking Chevrolet
18	22	Kyle Petty	Mello Yello Pontiac	39	40	Dick Trickle	Pedigree Food Chevrolet
19	32	Phil Parsons	Manheim Auctions Chevrolet	40	6	Todd Bodine	Factory Stores Ford
20	25	Jimmy Spencer	Meineke Mufflers Ford	41	36	Rich Bickle	Terminal Trucking Co. Ford
21	17	Derrike Cope	Bojangles' Ford				

After watching Mark Martin win his second successive NASCAR Winston Cup race Sunday, everyone headed for Indianapolis—and no one really knew what to expect. The date for the first NASCAR Winston Cup race at the most famous race track in the world had already been announced—and would take place a year hence.

Nine cars and drivers had headed for Indy last year after the Michigan race in a test session limited to a few invited teams.

But this year, invitations to the test session were given to the top 32 cars and drivers in the point standings. Last year, some 25,000 fans turned out to see the NASCAR stockers on the 2.5-mile oval for the first time.

This year, however, the Speedway was staffed up, and had announced that the two-day test would be open to fans for $5 per head. Speedway officials expected a big turnout. The question was just how many of the Midwest fans would be there.

Richard Petty finally got to make a lap or two around Indianapolis Motor Speedway—then he donated his car to the museum at the track.

Kenny Wallace's Dirt Devil Pontiac gets a tow back to Gasoline Alley after tagging the wall during the Indianapolis test session.

It didn't take long for the teams to find out. When the rigs arrived at the track late Sunday night after the drive from Michigan, the truck drivers were greeted like conquering heroes as they pulled into the IMS entrance. Hundreds of fans were on hand just to see the TRANSPORTERS!

That should have been an indication!

Mark Martin checked into the Speedway Motel, ordered his victory dinner—a pizza—and ended up sharing it and an hour of conversation with fans who saw the delivery man bring the pizza.

Monday morning, the line of fans seeking entrance to the Speedway stretched a half-mile at 7 a.m.—two hours before the gates would open. Although no head counts were given by the track, media members who cover the races at Indianapolis regularly estimated the crowd in excess of 75,000—EACH DAY!

The drivers responded to the fans' enthusiasm—and signed autograph after autograph. Many stood at the garage fence for more than an hour at a time, and many gave up their lunch breaks to go back to the fence to sign—and sign—and sign.

Over and over, fans were overheard saying, "You guys are so nice. We can't believe you come out here to sign for us. We could be here the whole month of May and maybe see one driver come out

here to sign autographs. You NASCAR guys are unbelievable! We can't wait until August next year."

Tony George and his IMS team can't wait either. After the two-day test, Indy announced it would open ticket sales to The Brickyard 400 NASCAR race scheduled for August 6, 1994. Within 36 hours, the entire Speedway was sold out! The race next August will be witnessed by the largest gathering of spectators ever to see a Winston Cup race!

For years, Richard Petty had hoped the Winston Cup cars would have a chance to run at Indianapolis. He had made many trips to The Brickyard (named for the 3.2 million bricks used as the original racing surface when the track was built in 1909) as a guest of STP when the Indy cars were making final preparations for the Indianapolis 500.

The NASCAR race date came two years too late for Richard to compete. But he still had the chance to put in a couple of "lukewarm" laps with an STP Pontiac on the final day of the test—and it was a special moment to see Richard back in a driver's suit, sliding through the window and then buckling up. When he was finished (turning laps just eight miles an hour slower than the regular

The Chevrolet Camaro pace car is set to turn the Winston Cup regulars loose during the inaugural practice session at Indianapolis Motor Speedway.

runners) he donated the Pontiac to the museum at the speedway.

Some of the NASCAR Winston Cup teams used the Indy test to work out combinations with new drivers for next year. Geoff Bodine spent his time with his Kulwicki Racing Ford—leaving Bud Moore to have a few laps turned in his Motorcraft Ford by Lake Speed and Morgan Shepherd—on loan from their own cars owned by Robert Yates and the Wood Brothers. Kyle Petty was going to make a few laps for Bud, as well, but couldn't get his long legs into the space left in the car by the way the seat was positioned for the much-shorter Bodine!

Terry Labonte worked with the Tide Chevrolet team and Ricky Rudd didn't make the trip to Indy. Billy Hagan had John Andretti in the Kellogg's Chevrolet, fueling talk he would have John as his regular driver for the 1994 season, if a sponsor could be found.

Ernie Irvan and the Morgan-McClure Kodak Lumina did not make the trip to Indy, either. Ernie had asked the Chevrolet owners for a release so he could become the full-time driver for Robert Yates Racing and things were at odds with the team.

The huge throng cheered everything that moved. Truck drivers were begged for autographs.

Crew members spent as much time as drivers signing everything a fan could carry. Drivers getting out of and into race cars drew cheers from fans hanging on the fence.

Midway through the second day, over a dozen cars lined up in the garage area to take to the track at the same time for an exhibition of running side-by-side around the track for the fans.

The first three laps were filled with position-swapping and tight drafting and the fans went wild, appreciating what the drivers were doing for them, and understanding that this was just a small taste of what would be coming next August.

On the fourth lap, however, John Andretti spun as he led the group of cars into the first turn. A wild game of dive-and-dodge ensued as drivers tried to find a way through the melee.

Jimmy Spencer and Mark Martin tangled and then hit Andretti, and suddenly the air had gone from the balloon. The fun was over, and Martin's team looked over the damaged Valvoline Ford, the car Mark had planned to run the next weekend at Bristol.

Despite the damaged cars, the teams and drivers, to a man, had enjoyed their two-day experience at The Brickyard. Heartened by the support shown by more than 150,000 fans over two days, the drivers all were eager to return in a year for a real race at the track.

As they exited the track, a fan held up a tee-shirt that said it all for everyone connected with the test session.

Emblazoned on the shirt under two side-by-side stock cars was the simple message:

"Door to Door in '94. Indianapolis."

BUD 500

BRISTOL INTERNATIONAL RACEWAY

AUGUST 28, 1993

*T*he August night race at Bristol has become one of the most anticipated by fans in the entire NASCAR Winston Cup schedule. It is a spectacle all want to attend—but most are forced to watch the event on ESPN. Every year, Larry Carrier adds more seats around the half-mile cereal bowl, and before they are built, the seats are sold, in a seemingly perpetual cycle!

Larry now can put more than 65,000 in Thunder Valley, and if he could find a way to double-deck the stands and double the capacity, he'd sell those seats, too. It's an amazing sight—and the action in the Friday night Busch Grand National and Saturday night Winston Cup races is absolutely non-stop.

The teams look forward to Bristol as well, particularly now that there is a way to get the transporters into the track. Teams don't have to work out of rental trucks or wait until the end of a practice session to head outside the track to the transporter and get a needed part or piece.

Bristol always signals the beginning of the final third of the season and drivers begin to cinch it up. Those who feel they have a chance for the championship begin to take things a little more seriously. Those who have yet to win a race begin to see the end of the season looming in the distance, and realize chances for that elusive victory get slimmer with each passing race.

Jack Roush, Mark and Arlene Martin and crew chief Steve Hmiel celebrate Martin's third-straight victory during the month of August.

The finish was decided by just over a car-length as Mark Martin held off a furiously-charging Rusty Wallace for the victory.

Rusty Wallace hoped to sweep Bristol in 1993, but he didn't have enough to beat Mark Martin this night.

And the Bud 500 is the first race of a string of successive races that will sort the real contenders for the title. It is this string of races that tests the organization of a race team in every aspect. Preparation, maintenance, morale, competitive fire and skills are all defined in the crucible that begins with Bristol.

This year, the string would be seven races, with teams racing every weekend for the next two months until Charlotte. From late August until early-October, the battle would be joined. Those trailing in points would not ask for leniency, and none would be given by those who had the lead.

Dale Earnhardt was firmly ensconced at the top of the point ladder. He had fought his way to a 259-point lead over "The Other Dale" Jarrett. Beginning with the Pepsi 400 at Daytona, Earnhardt had clobbered the competition. He had won three times in seven races, and at The Glen and at Michigan, had been good enough to run in the top three before problems.

Jarrett had put together an enviable string, too,

but had failed to get to victory lane. Since the Pepsi race, he had been out of the top eight just once—at The Glen. In that string, he had a trio of fourth places.

Mark Martin had been even more impressive. Back-to-back wins in the last two races came after a second, a third and a sixth. Only a 13th at Pocono marred his record in the last few outings.

He had climbed from tenth to fourth in the point standings as the teams headed for Bristol.

Rusty Wallace knew the time had come for him to try to make his run, if he had any hopes of bringing Miller and Pontiac a championship. He had fallen to 324 points behind, and for the black and yellow team, it was now or never.

Dick Trickle was standing in for Kenny Wallace at Bristol, with Kenny unable to go the distance after the Indy test injury. Busch Grand National regular Ward Burton's team announced it would move up to Winston Cup in 1995 with Hardee's upping its sponsorship level. And Citgo, Morgan Shepherd and the Wood Brothers announced they would be together in 1994. It was a fitting way to recognize the season put together by the group. Morgan was fifth in the point standings heading into Bristol, and had put 12 top-10 finishes on the board in 20 races.

Everyone was ready to begin the chase Friday morning. Too bad Mother Nature didn't want to watch cars on the track. A thunderstorm dumped 2.5 inches of rain on the track, turning the infield into Lake Larry. Saturday would be a full day, with practice and qualifying sessions slated prior to the start of the race.

Martin surprised himself by winning the pole on his race setup and with his race engine in the car. He said he had had the fastest car so many times and not won the pole that he had given up on

ing Ford ninth, just ahead of Harry Gant.

Where, you ask, was the point leader? Earnhardt qualified 19th—and would be forced to pit on the back side!

When the green flag dropped, it was evident that Martin was dialed in—and even more evident that Wallace was among the most determined drivers on the track. Mark led from the get-go, but soon Wallace had become the dominant car.

Martin's chances for a third-consecutive victory appeared gone when he pitted on lap 129 to have his crew tighten down a loose right rear tire. He lost two laps in the process and immediately

Derrike Cope had a tough night at the Bristol half-mile with Cale Yarborough's Bojangles' Ford.

thinking he could win one. Rusty Wallace, determined to continue his short-track excellence and make up some points on Earnhardt, qualified second, ahead of Ricky Rudd and a superb lap from rookie Bobby Labonte. Hut Stricklin and Rick Wilson surprised the field by qualifying fifth and sixth, with Derrike Cope and Jeff Gordon seventh and eighth. Jimmy Hensley put the Kulwicki Rac-

set about trying to get them back.

At the front, Wallace had everyone covered—and led 410 of the 500 laps in a display of dominance seldom seen on the circuit. Earnhardt fought a good fight, but pitting on the backstretch put him at a disadvantage on every pit stop.

The breaks went Martin's way during the race. He retrieved one of his lost laps when he profited from the Gordon/Cope altercation that brought out a yellow on lap 177.

He fought his way past Wallace again on lap 228—and then had to stay in front of the Pontiac driver until Dick Trickle spun 40 laps later and brought out the yellow that put Martin back on the lead lap.

Still, it would take more than 200 laps for Mark to find a way to deal with Wallace. Finally, with just 11 laps to go, Martin found the opening he needed—and went to the point for the first time since early in the race.

His work wasn't over. Wallace just would not quit. With Geoff and Brett Bodine fighting for seventh place just in front of the leaders, Martin was boxed. He was splitting his time looking out the windshield trying to find a way past the warring brothers—and looking in his mirror to try to block Wallace.

An exasperated Martin finally put the Valvo-line Ford's nose to Geoff Bodine in a "move-over" maneuver that left no doubt in anyone's mind what he meant. He managed to beat Wallace to the line by just over a car-length for his third-consecutive NASCAR Winston Cup win.

Earnhardt finished a solid third and Wallace had done his best, but picked up a mere 15 points for his efforts. Jarrett, on the other hand, lost the rear end in his car at the 200-lap mark, finished 31st—and fell to fourth place in the standings, behind Wallace and Martin. He now trailed by 354 and faced a huge uphill battle.

Wallace was now 309 behind and Martin trailed by 327. Earnhardt was beginning to look like a lock for his sixth championship.

As the teams left Bristol it was announced that in 1994 Goody's Headache Powders would become the title sponsorship for the April NASCAR Busch Grand National and August NASCAR Winston Cup events at Bristol.

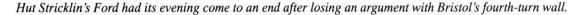

Hut Stricklin's Ford had its evening come to an end after losing an argument with Bristol's fourth-turn wall.

Rookie Jeff Gordon helped to bring Derrike Cope's night to an end at Bristol.

Fin. Pos.	Str. Pos.	Driver	Team	Fin. Pos.	Str. Pos.	Driver	Team
1	1	Mark Martin	Valvoline Ford	18	27	Jimmy Means	NAPA Ford
2	2	Rusty Wallace	Miller Genuine Draft Pontiac	19	28	Greg Sacks	Country Time Ford
3	19	Dale Earnhardt	GM Goodwrench Chevrolet	20	8	Jeff Gordon	DuPont Auto Finishes Chevrolet
4	10	Harry Gant	Skoal Bandit Chevrolet	21	22	Wally Dallenbach	Keystone Beer Ford
5	12	Rick Mast	Skoal Classic Ford	22	3	Ricky Rudd	Tide Chevrolet
6	9	Jimmy Hensley	Family Channel Ford	23	30	Sterling Marlin	Raybestos Ford
7	13	Brett Bodine	Quaker State Ford	24	26	Ken Schrader	Kodiak Chevrolet
8	11	Geoff Bodine	Motorcraft Ford	25	32	Jimmy Spencer	Meineke Mufflers Ford
9	23	Kenny Wallace	Dirt Devil Pontiac	26	34	Ernie Irvan	Kodak Film Chevrolet
10	24	Michael Waltrip	Pennzoil Pontiac	27	7	Derrike Cope	Bojangles' Ford
11	14	Bill Elliott	Budweiser Ford	28	6	Rick Wilson	STP Pontiac
12	31	Bobby Hillin	Heilig-Meyers Ford	29	17	Darrell Waltrip	Western Auto Chevrolet
13	16	Morgan Shepherd	Citgo Ford	30	20	Kyle Petty	Mello Yello Pontiac
14	25	Phil Parsons	Manheim Auctions Chevrolet	31	33	Dale Jarrett	Interstate Batteries Chevrolet
15	4	Bobby Labonte	Maxwell House Ford	32	5	Hut Stricklin	McDonald's Ford
16	21	Lake Speed	Havoline Ford	33	15	Bobby Hamilton	Fina Lube Ford
17	29	Dave Marcis	Tri-City Aviation Chevrolet	34	18	Terry Labonte	Kellogg's Chevrolet

MOUNTAIN DEW SOUTHERN 500

DARLINGTON RACEWAY

SEPTEMBER 5, 1993

Rick Mast and Darrell Waltrip lead rookie Jeff Gordon and Rusty Wallace in action at finicky Darlington.

*I*f there had been a reporter at Darlington who felt there were no new stories to tell, he must have arrived at the 1.366-mile track after spending the last month or so in a Biosphere!

The hottest item at the top of the list was the ongoing wrangling between Morgan-McClure Racing and Ernie Irvan. Any who thought Irvan would be in the Kodak Chevrolet for the Mountain Dew Southern 500 weekend had merely to wander over to the car or the transporter — and open his eyes.

Above the driver door was written Jeff Purvis. And Purvis' name was also on the transporter as the driver of the number four car.

After his fourth-consecutive triumph, Mark Martin shared victory lane with Miss Southern 500.

Little surprise then, when Ernie walked out in a black uniform for Friday practice and slid through the window of the Havoline Ford. Irvan would now be able to drive the Robert Yates Ford for the remainder of the new contract between the Texas oil company and Yates — through 1997.

Whither goest Lake Speed?

After doing a super job in the "28" since Watkins Glen, Lake was "ride-less" at Darlington, but it didn't take long for Bud Moore to announce that Lake had signed with him for the 1994 season.

Immediately, everyone started looking at the "7" car, wondering how long Jimmy Hensley would be there, and how soon Geoff Bodine would take over behind the wheel for the team he had purchased from Gerald Kulwicki in June.

Darlington announced the spring TranSouth 500 would revert to the 400-mile distance it had enjoyed from 1966-72, beginning with the March 1994 event. And track officials also announced the beginning of the long-anticipated "flip-flopping" of the start/finish line at the track in 1995. Immediately after the checkered flag fell on Sunday's Mountain Dew Southern 500, work would begin on the new backstretch tower, the first step toward "flopping" the track.

For the second week, Dick Trickle was standing by to relieve Kenny Wallace and Felix Sabates couldn't have been happier with his choice. Trickle had brought the Dirt Devil Pontiac to a ninth-place finish at Bristol, matching the best finish Kenny had posted for the team with his ninth at Watkins Glen.

Qualifying was beginning to have the same old result — for the sixth time this season, Kenny Schrader had held his breath the shortest time around the track and had grabbed the fastest time of the day.

Again this week, the front-row would be green and white — but it wasn't Brett Bodine on the outside of the front row. Harry Gant, the old Darlington-meister, had gone into his black bag of magic charms and found the right potion to sprinkle around the Skoal Chevrolet.

It was Harry's best qualifying effort of the year, and he needed it to just nip the most surprising qualifying run of the day. There must be something in the Labonte family genes that makes Darlington just a little 'ol rocking chair. Remember, this is where big brother Terry finished fourth in his first Southern 500—way back in ancient history in 1978. Was Bobby about to

Early in the race, Dale Earnhardt and Ernie Irvan waged a furious battle for the lead.

The Mountain Dew Southern 500 was the fourth event counting towards the Winston Million, but no driver was able to collect the big bonus in 1993.

join the "Iceman" with a new Darlington moniker?

Mark Martin just couldn't help himself. He was alternately grinning and stoic at Darlington. Grinning after three-straight victories — and iron-faced knowing the string would not go forever. He would start the race fourth.

Derrike Cope was a sparkling fifth, giving Cale Yarborough's team a chance to strut, and point-leader Dale Earnhardt let everyone know he wasn't interested in a back-lane pit this weekend, turning the sixth-fast time.

Bill Elliott and Rick Mast were seventh and eighth, with Sterling Marlin and Irvan, in his first ride with Yates, completing the top-ten.

Rusty Wallace, still seeking a way to cut into Earnhardt's huge lead, qualified 11th, but Dale Jarrett, still smarting from the rear-end failure at Bristol, continued his qualifying woes with a 27th-place start for Sunday's race.

After Darrell Waltrip was announced as president of the Unocal Darlington Record Club for the coming year, Irvan and Marlin were inducted as new members based on their qualifying times for last year's race.

Saturday night, Bobby Allison and the late Ray Hendrick were inducted into the National Motorsports Press Association's Hall of Fame in an emotion-filled ceremony.

Sunday morning, Martin was trying to put his game face on, but the grin kept slipping. He had locked the rest of the field out of the winner's circle the previous day in the Gatorade 200 Busch Grand National race. Going back to Watkins Glen, he had won every time he was belted into a car — either Busch or Cup. He was working on a five-race string, including two BGN's.

This boy wasn't warm, or scorching, or sizzling, or red-hot.

He was in the middle of a nuclear melt-down!

Martin and the rest of the competitors had plenty of time to prepare for the race. Heavy rain Sunday morning made it appear that the race might revert to its old date of Labor Day Monday. But after a three-hour delay, word came down from the NASCAR tower that a "weather window" existed. This race would start RIGHT NOW!

The drivers were ready—and none more ready than Earnhardt and Irvan. Dale was tired of hearing everyone say he was stroking his way to the title. And Irvan just couldn't wait to get the Havoline Ford to the front.

The two matched up early — and after a torrid struggle when they swapped the lead back and forth within the lap, each lap— wiser heads on pit road prevailed. Crew chiefs and team owners told each driver to use some sense early in the race. There was no reason to jeopardize a victory by wrecking within the first 50 laps!

Earnhardt and Martin then showed the crowd

how good they were. Between them, they led 279 of the 351 laps that would be run at the pioneer superspeedway that Sunday afternoon.

After spending the first half of the race battling, Martin finally took command of the race at lap 189, and was never out of the lead for the remainder — except for green-flag pit stops.

Surprisingly, there were only three cautions during the race—two for teams to check tire wear. Irvan spun to bring a natural caution—the final one of the race—with darkness gathering.

The yellow came out at lap 337—30 laps short of the 500-mile distance. And the decision-makers in the tower told teams that due to the waning light, there would be 10 laps left when the green flag flew. It would cut the race 16 laps short — but there was no choice, from a safety standpoint.

Martin was at the point, with Brett Bodine, Rusty Wallace and Earnhardt right behind him. Martin left no doubt who was going to win this one, blasting away from the contenders and leaving them to scrap for the left-overs.

And scrap they did. Brett looked in his mirror and saw the black "3", after Dale had gotten past Rusty. And in his effort to overtake the green Ford, Dale slipped and slapped the fourth-turn wall, falling to a fourth-place finish as Wallace got past in the final laps to take third. They were the only four cars on the lead lap.

Irvan came home fifth, battling with Rudd and Gant a lap down. Morgan Shepherd posted yet another top-10 finish in eighth, just ahead of pole-sitter Schrader. And Trickle gave Sabco its second-straight top-10, relief driving the Pontiac for Kenny Wallace.

In the gathering gloom, Mark Martin's grin was lit by enough internal candlepower to make auxiliary floodlights on the television cameras superfluous.

Four-straight NASCAR Winston Cup victories tend to create an incandescent smile.

Mark Martin and his Valvoline Ford were clearly in control throughout most of the Darlington afternoon.

164

Mark Martin's crew pitted him perfectly all afternoon at Darlington.

After sorting out all the problems, Ernie Irvan was all smiles after being named the driver of the future for Robert Yates' Havoline Fords.

Fin. Pos.	Str. Pos.	Driver	Team	Fin. Pos.	Str. Pos.	Driver	Team
1	4	Mark Martin	Valvoline Ford	21	34	Phil Parsons	Manheim Auctions Chevrolet
2	12	Brett Bodine	Quaker State Ford	22	15	Jeff Gordon	DuPont Auto Finishes Chevrolet
3	11	Rusty Wallace	Miller Genuine Draft Pontiac	23	26	Jimmy Hensley	Family Channel Ford
4	6	Dale Earnhardt	GM Goodwrench Chevrolet	24	19	Bobby Hillin	Heilig-Meyers Ford
5	10	Ernie Irvan	Havoline Ford	25	13	Greg Sacks	Country Time Ford
6	16	Ricky Rudd	Tide Chevrolet	26	22	Jeff Purvis	Kodak Film Chevrolet
7	2	Harry Gant	Skoal Bandit Chevrolet	27	17	Todd Bodine	Factory Stores Ford
8	21	Morgan Shepherd	Citgo Ford	28	24	Darrell Waltrip	Western Auto Chevrolet
9	1	Ken Schrader	Kodiak Chevrolet	29	33	Dave Marcis	STG Chevrolet
10	31	Kenny Wallace	Dirt Devil Pontiac	30	35	Rick Wilson	STP Pontiac
11	30	Wally Dallenbach	Keystone Ford	31	9	Sterling Marlin	Raybestos Brakes Ford
12	27	Dale Jarrett	Interstate Batteries Chevrolet	32	8	Rick Mast	Skoal Classic Ford
13	25	Michael Waltrip	Pennzoil Pontiac	33	20	Terry Labonte	Kellogg's Chevrolet
14	3	Bobby Labonte	Maxwell House Ford	34	18	Ted Musgrave	Jasper Engines Ford
15	14	Jimmy Spencer	Meineke Mufflers Ford	35	36	Mike Skinner	Means Racing Ford
16	28	Kyle Petty	Mello Yello Pontiac	36	23	Hut Stricklin	McDonald's Ford
17	5	Derrike Cope	Bojangles' Ford	37	40	H.B. Bailey	Almeda Auto Parts Pontiac
18	7	Bill Elliott	Budweiser Ford	38	38	Brad Teague	Ball Motorsports Chevrolet
19	32	Bobby Hamilton	Fina Lube Ford	39	39	Jimmy Means	Means Racing Ford
20	29	Geoff Bodine	Motorcraft Ford				

MILLER GENUINE DRAFT 400

RICHMOND INTERNATIONAL RACEWAY

SEPTEMBER 11, 1993

Darrell Waltrip had the best run of his season, but at the end, Rusty Wallace would move past to win, while Mark Martin finished sixth. Darrell was seventh.

*E*ntering the third race in the seven-event swing, Rusty Wallace, Mark Martin and Dale Jarrett faced an uphill battle. Their dreams of a NASCAR Winston Cup season were still sugarplums dancing in their heads — but the black-clad team from Welcome, NC, had answered their every challenge.

Sure, Martin had finished out of the top-three only once since the Pepsi 400 at Daytona, including a second, a third and four-straight victories. He'd climbed from 10th to third in the standings. But despite his torrid string of races, he still was 307 points behind Dale Earnhardt.

Dale Jarrett had some trouble during the same races, losing a rear end at Bristol and having clutch failure at The Glen. He had dropped from the runner-up position in the point standings and now was fourth, 392 points behind. Something good had to happen to keep the Daytona

Jimmy Hensley did a superb job of driving for the Alan Kulwicki Racing team during the summer. Richmond would be his last race in the Ford.

166

500 by STP winner in the hunt.

Wallace could not have been happier than he was at Richmond. He had been in rocket ships at every short-track event during the season, winning three of the first five races at the bullrings and finishing second in the other two by a total of less than five car lengths. Since the Pepsi 400, he had been out of the top-three finishers just three times

would have lived up to its new moniker.

Martin's combined Busch and Winston Cup win streak had now climbed to six, and although Mark kept saying he expected the streak to end, he was doing his best to add his name to another page of the NASCAR Winston Cup record book. If he could win at Richmond, he would become the first driver in the modern era (since 1972) to

Rusty Wallace snapped Mark Martin's four-race winning streak with his sixth victory of the season at Richmond.

—and one of those was a sixth. He claimed a "moral victory"-17th at Talladega on the lead lap and was 19th at The Glen after losing a cylinder while in a position to challenge for the win in the final laps.

His car sponsor was also the race sponsor, and Wallace carried good feelings to Richmond. His mount was a car formerly known to the team as "Midnight," re-skinned by the team and renamed "Midnight Rider." With Richmond running under its lights, and the weekend named "Showdown at Sundown," Wallace hoped by midnight his car

win five consecutive races.

What about the point-leader? Already people were beginning to talk about Earnhardt locking up the championship as early as Charlotte.

Earnhardt had been through this before. He knew that with eight races to go, anything could happen — and probably would! He'd gone through the first two-thirds of the season remarkably trouble-free, and everyone on the team knew about the law of averages in NASCAR Winston Cup racing. He'd had engine failure at Martinsville in the spring, but other than that, his luck had been remarkable.

Not only had his car been fast — no one questioned that part after six point-race victories and The Winston win — but Andy Petree and the rest

of the team also had made his Goodwrench Chevrolets the most reliable on the circuit. Heading into Richmond, Earnhardt had completed 99.11 percent of all the laps run in the 22 races already on the books!

Bill Elliott desperately needed a break. But his team appeared to be starting to click better than early in the season. Since the Pepsi 400, he had finished third at Pocono and fourth at The Glen and had been hovering around the top-ten in four other events. He had moved from 16th in the point standings to 11th, and the pride of the Junior Johnson-owned team was at stake. Elliott and the team wanted an invitation to the stage at the Waldorf — and they would have to be in the top-ten at season's end if that was to happen.

Mark Martin had fashioned a remarkable record in Busch racing this year. If his Winn-Dixie Ford finished the race, it won. And he had the black car ready for Friday night at Richmond in hopes of continuing the string. He belted in — and won again, for his fifth Busch win of the year — and stretched his combined Busch/Cup mark to seven-straight.

Many on pit road had conceded the Busch

Pole for the NASCAR Winston Cup race to Ken Schrader. After all, he had six of them already this season and was the leader for the year-end Busch bonus. All expected Ernie Irvan and Martin to be fast, along with Rusty, but no one paid attention to the blue Ford over in the corner on the far side of the garage.

Not until qualifying, that is. And when the session was completed, Bobby Labonte had become the first Rookie of the Year candidate to win a pole since Davey Allison won five in 1987.

Labonte surprised everyone — including himself — in becoming the tenth-different pole winner of the season, and qualifying the Maxwell House Ford for the 1994 Busch Clash at Daytona.

The rookie's lap knocked Irvan off the pole, but it would be a Ford front-row, just ahead of Wallace and Darrell Waltrip, who had his best qualifying lap of the season. Waltrip could have been expected to run well at Richmond. In the spring race, he had qualified fifth. The Skoal Kids, Harry Gant and Rick Mast, made up the third row, with Geoff Bodine and Dale Earnhardt in row four.

Dick Trickle turned in an excellent performance in the Ruolo Brothers Pedigree Dog Food Chevrolet to start ninth. Martin would start 10th in search of his fifth-straight win.

Richmond under the lights is something special and Paul Sawyer and his boys, Wayne and Bill, provide one of the most modern and intriguing arenas on the tour. The .75-mile track incorporates short-track corners with some superspeedway characteristics, and it provides excellent competition. The largest crowds to see a sporting event in Virginia (75,000-plus) turn out for the race and due to Paul's planning, there's not a bad seat anywhere in the house.

The first quarter of the race it looked like a Darrell Waltrip and Rusty Wallace showdown was shaping up, but that began to fade after Darrell used his brakes more than anticipated in the head-to-head struggle with Rusty.

By the 100-lap mark, however, Martin's familiar Valvoline Ford was at the point, and the Arkansas native appeared headed for his fifth-straight victory. He just hooked up and checked out from the field, leaving the remainder of the competitors to battle for what appeared to be second place yet another week.

Martin was so far ahead that the team checked up and stopped running as hard — and then the track changed, and with it, Lady Luck decided she'd put in enough seat time with Martin.

On lap 267, she thumbed a ride with Rusty, and he was more than happy to let her in the cockpit with him. Rusty kept his lead for the remainder of the race, but a late-race caution with just 18 laps to go kept it interesting. On the restart, Gant spun and collected Bobby Hillin while Ted Musgrave and Rick Mast got together. The yellow was back out, with the green waving with just eight laps to go.

In Rusty's mirror was Elliott, with Earnhardt, Ricky Rudd, Martin, Jeff Gordon and others in trail. Rusty knew Elliott was desperate for a win, and wanted Earnhardt kept right where he was. Wallace

was picture-perfect at the drop of the green. He jumped away, and left Earnhardt and Elliott to duel for second place. Then Trickle hit the wall, the yellow came out with four to go, and the green waved again for a two-lap shoot-out. Again, Rusty hit the mark perfectly, and Elliott held off Earnhardt for his best finish of the season.

The win was his sixth for the season, but Wallace gained just 20 points on Earnhardt. Martin had failed to win his fifth-straight Cup race, but was still third in points, falling to sixth at the end of the race. Dale Jarrett's hopes were all but gone. His 14th-place finish dropped him to 436 behind Earnhardt.

Ricky Rudd recovered from this spin to finish fourth at Richmond, his "home" track.

The grin tells it all. Rusty Wallace had won his sixth race of the season, beating Bill Elliott by more than a half-second.

Fin. Pos.	Str. Pos.	Driver	Team	Fin. Pos.	Str. Pos.	Driver	Team
1	3	Rusty Wallace	Miller Genuine Draft Pontiac	19	15	Michael Waltrip	Pennzoil Pontiac
2	26	Bill Elliott	Budweiser Ford	20	27	Phil Parsons	Manheim Auctions Chevrolet
3	8	Dale Earnhardt	GM Goodwrench Chevrolet	21	19	Jimmy Hensley	Cellular One Ford
4	17	Ricky Rudd	Tide Chevrolet	22	35	Ted Musgrave	Jasper Engines Ford
5	16	Brett Bodine	Quaker State Ford	23	33	Dave Marcis	Swanson Frozen Foods Chevrolet
6	10	Mark Martin	Valvoline Ford	24	24	Sterling Marlin	Raybestos Brakes Ford
7	4	Darrell Waltrip	Western Auto Chevrolet	25	9	Dick Trickle	Pedigree Food for Dogs Chevrolet
8	23	Terry Labonte	Kellogg's Chevrolet	26	31	Jimmy Means	Means Racing Ford
9	11	Kyle Petty	Mello Yello Pontiac	27	34	Bobby Hillin	Heilig-Meyers Ford
10	22	Jeff Gordon	DuPont Auto Finishes Chevrolet	28	14	Derrike Cope	Bojangles' Ford
11	5	Harry Gant	Skoal Bandit Chevrolet	29	20	Rick Wilson	STP Pontiac
12	12	Ken Schrader	Kodiak Chevrolet	30	29	Morgan Shepherd	Citgo Ford
13	1	Bobby Labonte	Maxwell House Ford	31	36	Greg Sacks	Country Time Ford
14	13	Dale Jarrett	Interstate Batteries Chevrolet	32	28	Kenny Wallace	Dirt Devil Pontiac
15	30	Wally Dallenbach	Keystone Beer Ford	33	32	Todd Bodine	Factory Stores Ford
16	18	Jeff Purvis	Kodak Film Chevrolet	34	7	Geoff Bodine	Motorcraft Ford
17	25	Hut Stricklin	McDonald's Ford	35	21	Jimmy Spencer	Meineke Mufflers Ford
18	6	Rick Mast	Skoal Classic Ford	36	2	Ernie Irvan	Havoline Ford

SPLITFIRE SPARK PLUG 500

***DOVER DOWNS
INTERNATIONAL SPEEDWAY***

SEPTEMBER 19, 1993

Jeff Gordon had a great qualifying run to start in the second row, but car problems led to a 24th-place finish.

A s far as Rusty Wallace was concerned, it was "Showtime." Mark Martin's four-race winning streak was history. Wallace had won his sixth race of the season at Richmond, and he faced the final two short-track races of the season in the coming two weekends. He felt confident he could gain points on Dale Earnhardt at Martinsville and North Wilkesboro.

His biggest concern was Dover. He had run well at Denis Glynn's "Monster Mile" in the past, but had never been to victory lane at Dover. In fact, he had to look around to see where it was, just in case he needed it at the end of the day on Sunday.

*Tony Glover intently watches
his new driver, Jeff Purvis.*

Few thought at the beginning of the 1993 season that a single driver would win a half-dozen races. The season had looked, on paper, like it would be one incredible parity — when a driver who won three or four races and had solid finishes in other events would become the 1993 NASCAR Winston Cup Champion.

But here the teams were, unloading their charges for the 24th race of the season, and already a pair of drivers had won a half-dozen events. Earnhardt and Wallace, in the blackest of the black cars on the circuit this year, had surprised the pundits. Martin and his red, white and blue Valvoline Ford had been the only other driver to post multiple wins while Dale and Rusty were hogging the checkered flags.

Before Martin began his tear at The Glen, the Manufacturer's Championship had been a runaway for Chevrolet. The Bowtie Brigade had notched 129 points, with defending champion Ford trailing badly with only 102 points. With Ford behind by 27 points, it appeared that Chevrolet would be awarded the coveted title at the New York awards banquet.

But Martin's victories had narrowed the score, and Rusty's win, coupled with Elliott's sterling finish the previous weekend at Richmond, had turned the battle for Detroit bragging rights into a dogfight again. Entering Dover, Chevrolet was still the leader, but the gap had closed considerably. The Blue Ovals were only six points behind, 153-147, with Pontiac now third at 137. Try as he had, Rusty had not been able to single-handedly bring Pontiac the title. He had little help from his fellow Pontiac drivers.

For the second time in as many races, Ernie Irvan had qualified second-fastest, but after Bobby Labonte's heroics at Richmond, this time Wallace left no doubt he had a car capable of scoring yet another victory. When qualifying was over, the Miller Pontiac would start from the pole for the first time since the April Bristol race.

Funny things seem to happen when drivers are in the home territory of their sponsors. Ernie Irvan blistered the track at Watkins Glen, with Kodak's employees on hand, while he drove the Morgan-

Darrell Waltrip's pit crew goes to work. Waltrip finished in third place after starting 17th.

174

McClure Chevrolet.

This time it would be Jeff Gordon, who gave the DuPont execs and employees something to brag about during the weekend. The rookie qualified his Hendrick-owned Chevrolet third-fastest, with Geoff Bodine making his debut behind the wheel of his Family Channel Ford on the outside of the second row.

Bodine and Bud Moore had split immediately following the Richmond race, and Bodine took over the seat of the Kulwicki Racing Ford, easing Jimmy Hensley out the door. That put Lake Speed into the Motorcraft Ford for the remainder of the season as Bud's team hoped to get a head-start on 1994.

Martin and Rick Wilson qualified fifth and sixth, with Wilson hoping to turn around the off season through which the Petty Enterprises STP Pontiac had suffered. Morgan Shepherd and Harry Gant made up the fourth row, with point-leader Earnhardt ninth and Kenny Schrader on the outside of the fifth row.

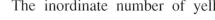

In Friday's practice, Brett Bodine lost a freeze plug from the engine in his Quaker State Ford which allowed water to exit the block - and when his tires hit the water, Brett slipped into the third-turn wall. With a broken right wrist, Brett headed to find Dr. Terry Trammel, the orthopedic surgeon who works with many IndyCar and NASCAR drivers, while Dick "Mr. Substitute" Trickle was pressed into service in the back-up green and white Ford.

More than 86,000 fans were on hand — the biggest crowd in the history of Delaware at a sporting event — but few expected the shape the Splitfire 500 would take as the Sunday afternoon progressed.

The shape was yellow — and rectangular — and it waved from the start/finish flagstand on a regular basis during this September afternoon. Some of the cautions were "natural" yellows — coming from incidents on the track. Others were "safety" yellows, used by NASCAR for teams to check tire wear.

The inordinate number of yellow

Rusty Wallace brings the field down the front stretch at Dover. Wallace held off a hard-charging Ken Schrader for the win.

flags (16) kept the racing tight for the fans — and helped Wallace return from two laps down to challenge for victory.

Wallace, with a tire going down, pitted on lap 283 and lost two laps while his crew replaced his Goodyear Eagles. He made up one of those laps, but was still a lap in arrears to the leaders when another caution emerged.

The race went back to green. Two laps later, Wallace got back in the tail of the lead lap, moving past Schrader. When Ted Musgrave's engine blew up on lap 402, Wallace made up his lap and was on equal terms with the other seven drivers on the lead lap.

Rusty still had work to do, and finally, with 20 laps to go, he took over the point and held off a determined rush by Schrader to win his seventh race of the year.

After work on their cars, Dale Earnhardt, Ricky Rudd and Jeff Gordon all returned to the race, trying to salvage as many points as possible. Earnhardt, however, was classified 27th in the final results, and that, combined with Wallace's second-straight victory, cut 103 points off Earnhardt's lead.

Wallace now trailed by 181 points and felt he had a chance. There were six races left — and Alan Kulwicki had rallied from 278 behind following Dover to win the title last year.

Martin had his problems. He hit the wall and was out of the race before half-distance. Dale Jarrett's dimly-flickering title hopes got a boost from Earnhardt's problems. Jarrett finished fourth and gained 83 points — but he was still far behind.

After finally moving into the top-10 in the point standings after his second place at Richmond the week before, Bill Elliott could manage only a lap-down tenth place at Dover. The Richmond runner-up momentum had not carried over to Delaware.

Bobby Labonte continued his hot streak, finishing seventh and grabbing another top-10 position in his battle for the rookie title.

Bud Moore, a true legend in the sport of NASCAR Winston Cup racing, checks the time of Lake Speed.

176

A dejected Hut Stricklin walks back to the pits after this incident eliminated both he and Dale Earnhardt.

Fin. Pos.	Str. Pos.	Driver	Team	Fin. Pos.	Str. Pos.	Driver	Team
1	1	Rusty Wallace	Miller Genuine Draft Pontiac	20	29	Greg Sacks	Country Time Ford
2	10	Ken Schrader	Kodiak Chevrolet	21	22	Ricky Rudd	Tide Chevrolet
3	17	Darrell Waltrip	Western Auto Chevrolet	22	30	Jimmy Horton	Active Trucking Service Chevrolet
4	26	Dale Jarrett	Interstate Batteries Chevrolet	23	24	Michael Waltrip	Pennzoil Pontiac
5	8	Harry Gant	Skoal Bandit Chevrolet	24	3	Jeff Gordon	DuPont Auto Finishes Chevrolet
6	19	Jimmy Spencer	Meineke Mufflers Ford	25	23	Dick Trickle	Quaker State Ford
7	11	Bobby Labonte	Maxwell House Ford	26	2	Ernie Irvan	Havoline Ford
8	27	Terry Labonte	Kellogg's Chevrolet	27	9	Dale Earnhardt	GM Goodwrench Chevrolet
9	7	Morgan Shepherd	Citgo Ford	28	21	Ted Musgrave	Jasper Engines Ford
10	13	Bill Elliott	Budweiser Ford	29	16	Hut Stricklin	McDonald's Ford
11	18	Sterling Marlin	Raybestos Brakes Ford	30	4	Geoff Bodine	Family Channel Ford
12	32	Bobby Hillin	Heilig-Meyers Ford	31	5	Mark Martin	Valvoline Ford
13	35	Jeff Purvis	Kodak Film Chevrolet	32	14	Derrike Cope	Bojangles' Ford
14	15	Kyle Petty	Mello Yello Pontiac	33	25	Lake Speed	Motorcraft Ford
15	33	Wally Dallenbach	Keystone Beer Ford	34	6	Rick Wilson	STP Pontiac
16	36	Kenny Wallace	Dirt Devil Pontiac	35	28	Todd Bodine	Factory Stores Ford
17	37	Jimmy Means	Hurley Limo Ford	36	34	Bob Schacht	Queenstown Harbor Chevrolet
18	12	Rick Mast	Skoal Classic Ford	37	20	Phil Parsons	Manheim Auctions Chevrolet
19	31	Dave Marcis	Tina & Alan Chevrolet				

GOODY'S 500

MARTINSVILLE SPEEDWAY   *SEPTEMBER 26, 1993*

It's a Ford front row as Ernie Irvan and Geoff Bodine prepare to take the green flag.

When he's pumped, Rusty Wallace's enthusiasm knows no boundaries. So when he came be-bopping into Clay Earles' beautiful Martinsville Speedway, Wallace was, in his own words, "jacked."

He was at full rev. Words didn't come out of his mouth in phrases or tumble out in sentences. Rusty opened his mouth, and entire paragraphs came flying out in a stream of consciousness. His team had worked hard all week in the shop. They believed the championship was far from over — and that finally, they had a shot. Dale Earnhardt had finally had some bad luck and had a poor finish at Dover, and Rusty's team had capitalized.

Now they were at the short tracks for the next two races, and their record was unsurpassed this year. In six races, they had won four and

NASCAR officials keep a close eye on the action as the majority of the field stops in the pits for service.

Rusty Wallace and Mark Martin pause to discuss track conditions at Martinsville.

finished second twice. Yes, one might say they were ready.

Next door, in the Goodwrench transporter, no one was licking any wounds — or running scared from Wallace. Richard Childress' team took the Dover debacle in stride. One minute they had been running second, with a real chance of putting Wallace's challenge on the shelf. The next, they were in the garage, doing yeoman's work to get the black Chevrolet back on the track.

Still, the point lead was 181 — and to these guys, 181 is like 1801. Earnhardt's team has no quit in them. They had set out to return to the front this year, and no little problem at Dover would derail that express.

In the week that had passed since Dover, Rick Wilson had begun his search for a ride for 1994. Wally Dallenbach would finish out the season with Jack Roush and then move into the Petty Enterprises car.

Harry Melling had moved his race team from Dawsonville, GA, to North Carolina, where the team moved into the recently vacated space owned by Bob Rahilly near Charlotte. When Butch Mock

and Rahilly had separated earlier in the month, Mock had moved the team to another shop.

The championship battle had seemingly come down to just two teams.

Despite Mark Martin's four-straight wins, Dover had punished the Valvoline Ford driver. He was now a distant third in the points, and with six races remaining, trailed by 329 with little real chance of challenging for the title.

Dale Jarrett had done his best at Dover, and had gained points. But now, 353 points behind, the Daytona winner was watching Martin ahead of him and Morgan Shepherd behind him, trying to protect his fourth place — and perhaps move up to third or even second by the end of the season.

Davey Allison had never won at Martinsville, nor had his father. So, prior to the spring race, Davey and the Robert Yates team had spent three days testing at Martinsville in hopes of finding a combination that would work. After more than 700 laps, improvements were found, and Davey qualified second and finished sixth in his best career outing there. Crew chief Larry McReynolds brought the black book back to Martinsville and

Ernie Irvan became the real beneficiary of the intensive test session.

When qualifying was completed at the half-mile Virginia oval, Ernie had earned the first pole of the year for Robert Yates Racing. Geoff Bodine was right beside him, and it was still taking some time for fans in the crowd to identify the two drivers with the "28" and "7" cars after years in the "4" and the "15."

Sterling Marlin, who blew a motor in the final laps of practice before qualifying, found his back-up motor just as good, and turned the third-fastest lap. Wallace was right at home in this week's edition of the Miller rocket, and would start fourth. Kyle Petty returned to the front of the field with the fifth-quickest lap, and Darrell Waltrip was telling anyone who would listen that he had the best car in the field after he was sixth-fastest. He later virtually guaranteed he would win the race two days hence.

Dale Earnhardt was seventh for the start, with Jimmy Hensley showing his local knowledge of the track by putting the Petty Enterprises Pontiac eighth-fastest. He was in the car while Rick Wilson recovered from sore ribs.

Completing the top-10 were Bobby Labonte with another solid effort, and Todd Bodine, showing his Busch lessons at Martinsville had been well-learned.

When Sunday's race took the flag in front of a sold-out crowd, the event took on three storylines. First was Irvan's domination of the race, where he led seemingly at will throughout the 500-lap distance. In all, he had the Havoline Ford at the point for 402

Jimmy Hensley, who was knocked out of the race in a final-lap mishap, substitutes for an ailing Kyle Petty.

of the laps, and breezed home the winner by more than two seconds — one of the largest margins of victory the entire season!

The second was Dale Earnhardt's gritty performance that ended in disaster. Earnhardt, who suffered slight damage early in the race during a pit-road altercation with Darrell Waltrip, battled his way all the way back to fifth place — and then had the rear-end in his Goodwrench Chevrolet give up the ghost. Earnhardt was classified 29th.

The third was the near-perfect performance, once again, of Rusty Wallace, who took advantage of Earnhardt's misfortune. When you trail by 181 points and your adversary has a problem, it's not enough just to grab points by trying to finish. The way to obtain the maximum points is to push on and use that opportunity to gain the most. And that's just what Wallace did.

He led early in the race for the five extra

points, and although he didn't win or lead the most laps, Wallace did continue his superb season on the short tracks, finishing second to Ernie. Jimmy Spencer drove a superb race to finish third, ahead of Ricky Rudd. Rudd's performance was particularly gratifying because he had battled from the back-side pit road all day, and had been on the lead lap throughout the race. A win would have been better for the Virginian, but he was plenty proud of

morning quarterbacking was about to begin. Earnhardt had stumbled — twice in a row. One was not his fault — and the second was mechanical. No matter. Wallace had come from 309 behind to now trail by 82 with five races left.

Dale Jarrett kept hanging in there, finishing fifth and using Earnhardt's problems to gain 79 points. That, combined with Mark Martin's 16th place, moved Jarrett into third place in the point

his fourth place after a grueling, humid afternoon.

While Irvan was celebrating his first victory with the Robert Yates crew in victory lane — and emotionally peeling off his black driving suit to proudly display a Davey Allison tee shirt he wore under it — Wallace was counting points.

His second-place finish, combined with Earnhardt's 29th, meant a net gain of 99 points. The margin was now down to 82 points between the two — and suddenly, after all the talking, there was a point race for the NASCAR Winston Cup.

All the "woulda, coulda, shoulda" Monday

Jeff Purvis was able to recover from this spin to finish in the 17th position after starting 30th.

standings, 16 markers ahead of Martin.

Wallace was seen sky-walking his way over the cars lined up exiting Martinsville. If he had been "jacked" when he got to Martinsville 181 behind, what would he call himself at North Wilkesboro when he trailed by just 82?

Darrell Waltrip gets out of shape, allowing a string of cars to slip by on the lower side of the track.

Fin. Pos.	Str. Pos.	Driver	Team	Fin. Pos.	Str. Pos.	Driver	Team
1	1	Ernie Irvan	Havoline Ford	18	6	Darrell Waltrip	Western Auto Chevrolet
2	4	Rusty Wallace	Miller Genuine Draft Pontiac	19	33	Phil Parsons	Manheim Auctions Chevrolet
3	15	Jimmy Spencer	Meineke Mufflers Ford	20	18	Derrike Cope	Bojangles' Ford
4	20	Ricky Rudd	Tide Chevrolet	21	32	Dave Marcis	Metts Tours Chevrolet
5	17	Dale Jarrett	Interstate Batteries Chevrolet	22	26	Bobby Hillin	Heilig-Meyers Ford
6	14	Brett Bodine	Quaker State Ford	23	16	Hut Stricklin	McDonald's Ford
7	29	Terry Labonte	Kellogg's Chevrolet	24	19	Lake Speed	Motorcraft Ford
8	24	Michael Waltrip	Pennzoil Pontiac	25	10	Todd Bodine	Factory Stores Ford
9	11	Morgan Shepherd	Citgo Ford	26	13	Rick Mast	Skoal Classic Ford
10	5	Kyle Petty	Mello Yello Pontiac	27	31	Wally Dallenbach	Keystone Beer Ford
11	25	Jeff Gordon	DuPont Auto Finishes Chevrolet	28	34	Greg Sacks	Country Time Ford
12	22	Bill Elliott	Budweiser Ford	29	7	Dale Earnhardt	GM Goodwrench Chevrolet
13	12	Ken Schrader	Kodiak Chevrolet	30	3	Sterling Marlin	Raybestos Brakes Ford
14	2	Geoff Bodine	Family Channel Ford	31	28	Ted Musgrave	Jasper Engines Ford
15	23	Kenny Wallace	Dirt Devil Pontiac	32	9	Bobby Labonte	Maxwell House Ford
16	21	Mark Martin	Valvoline Ford	33	27	Harry Gant	Skoal Bandit Chevrolet
17	30	Jeff Purvis	Kodak Film Chevrolet	34	8	Jimmy Hensley	STP Pontiac

TYSON HOLLY FARMS 400

Ernie Irvan may have proven there was a new winner on the block with his powerful victory at Martinsville the weekend before, but nothing was about to cut into the gritty determination Rusty Wallace brought to North Wilkesboro.

For the first 24 races of the season, Wallace had been his jocular self. He had done his high-flying stint at Daytona and Talladega, recovered from a broken wrist and watched his hopes for a second NASCAR Winston Cup all but disappear when he had plummeted to 333 points behind after the DieHard 500 just seven races ago.

But the fire in his belly hadn't been extinguished. And the string of five consecutive top-three finishes, including a pair of wins, had fanned the fire into an inferno. He called himself "dedicated" to winning

Although they are fierce competitors on the track, Rusty Wallace and Dale Earnhardt remain close friends.

Crew members of the Texaco Havoline Ford use spare tires for seats while monitoring Ernie Irvan's track position.

the championship. Others began to call him "obsessed." When asked about it, he briefly let a wry grin slide onto his face. "Let 'em call it whatever they want. We are making every effort we can to win this title, now that we've gotten within striking distance of Dale."

If Rusty and his team were fiercely determined, you can imagine what was going on with Dale Earnhardt's team. In workman-like fashion, the "Flying Aces" just kept digging. After all, they

very interesting on every front!

When the teams unloaded at Enoch Staley's .625-mile oval nestled in North Carolina's Brushy Mountains, there was a new name over the door on Larry Hedrick's Manheim Auctions Chevrolet.

Phil Parsons, who had posted the only top-10 finish in the team's history, had been released and

The crowd rises to its feet in anticipation of a restart.

were still the point leaders. They weren't doing the chasing. They were the ones who would have to be caught — and the pressures of title runs in the past gave them the experience they needed to just keep on keeping on — and waiting until the race was over to count points.

With Ford's five victories in the last seven races, and Pontiac's trips to victory lane in the other two, the battle for the Manufacturer's championship continued to tighten. Chevrolet was clinging to a three-point lead, 163-160, over the Blue Ovals, but Pontiac had pulled back into a contending position with 152 points.

With just five races remaining, it was getting

Dick Trickle, after playing "Have Helmet, Will Travel" for the last five races, had found a home for the remainder of the season. Hedrick was hopeful of having Busch Grand National regular Robert Pressley in his car for the 1994 season, but in the meantime, would finish out the season with Trickle, acknowledged as one of the best chassis men in the business.

Most of the eyes in the crowd were focused, however, on the black cars in the garage. Wallace had compiled one of the most outstanding records in NASCAR history on the short tracks during the 1993 season. In seven outings, he had won four times, and finished second the other three. This

was the final event on a bullring for the year, and Rusty had his usual Miller Meteor in the garage.

Through the years, Earnhardt had been a short-track terror. Of his 59 career victories, 30 had come on the bullrings. But he hadn't won at Bristol, North Wilkesboro, Richmond or Martinsville since he snapped Harry Gant's four-race winning streak here in October two years ago. This would be his last chance to avoid being shut-out on the short tracks for the second-straight year — something that had never happened to him in his career.

The other black car getting the eye was Irvan. Particularly after qualifying.

For the fourth time in five races, Irvan had slapped the Havoline Thunderbird on the front row — and for the second-straight race, would have the chance to win from the pole. His qualifying time was not a track record, but it was more than fast enough to earn his fourth pole position of the season, tying him with Mark Martin for second

place behind Ken Schrader's six poles.

Ricky Rudd would start outside the black Ford on the front row, with Kyle Petty getting another black car revved up for an excellent third starting position. Terry Labonte was fourth-fastest in Billy Hagan's Kellogg's car, and John Andretti made the field in Hagan's second car, squeaking in 31st. Harry Gant and Martin made up the third row, with Darrell Waltrip still looking for his first win of the year in seventh place for the start.

Bill Elliott, hoping to notch his first win of the year at Junior Johnson's "home" track, qualified eighth-fastest, with Sterling Marlin and Dale Earnhardt completing the top-ten. Right behind Earnhardt was Wallace, where he could see the point-leader through his windshield.

Before the race, Rusty admitted the best thing he could do to guarantee a point gain would be to lead the most laps and win the race. And when the green flag dropped, he set out to do just that.

Some of his challengers would feel the bite of North Wilkesboro, with 13 cars suffering damage in a first-lap melee.

Among them were Jeff Gordon, Morgan Shepherd, Geoff Bodine, Derrike Cope, Hut Stricklin, Lake Speed, Todd Bodine, Ted Musgrave, Kenny Schrader, John Andretti, Martin, Elliott — and Earnhardt.

For some, the problem would turn out to be just sheet metal damage, and Earnhardt was one of those.

After his crew pulled the metal away from the wheel openings, Earnhardt was ready to charge to the front — and as he did, Wallace played tagalong, shrewdly following through the holes Dale carved.

By lap 79, Wallace felt he was ready to get

laps to go, Wallace took a desperate risk, making a hole between Gant and Cope in the middle of the first and second turns, and got through. Earnhardt was trapped behind the green and yellow cars, and couldn't clear traffic and mount a challenge in the remaining laps.

The margin of victory at the end of the 400-lapper was just over 1.6 seconds. Wallace had done what he needed to. He had picked up another ten points on Earnhardt, despite Dale's superb performance. The margin was now down to 72 points between the pair of friendly rivals.

Irvan came home in third place with another strong showing in Robert Yates' Ford. Kyle Petty returned to the front with a hard-fought fourth place, the only other car able to complete the distance on the lead lap. Rudd was fifth, a lap in ar-

Bill Elliott's Budweiser Thunderbird, showing some contact on the nose, receives some quick service.

past the black Chevrolet and he dove under Dale in the fourth turn. He continued to the front, and Earnhardt faded slightly.

Rusty finally moved to the point on the 159th lap, and went on to lead a total of 182 laps to gain the five bonus points for leading the most laps.

Earnhardt wouldn't go away, however. He fought his way back to second place and a spirited battle between the two ensued. Finally, with 18

rears.

The final race of the seven-event marathon was next. And teams would have to try to figure out the handling of their cars with the spoiler and ride-height changes NASCAR had mandated for Charlotte.

Kyle Petty was in the thick of things all afternoon. Petty finished the day in fourth place.

Fin. Pos.	Str. Pos.	Driver	Team	Fin. Pos.	Str. Pos.	Driver	Team
1	11	Rusty Wallace	Miller Genuine Draft Pontiac	18	8	Bill Elliott	Budweiser Ford
2	10	Dale Earnhardt	GM Goodwrench Chevrolet	19	9	Sterling Marlin	Raybestos Brakes Ford
3	1	Ernie Irvan	Havoline Ford	20	27	Derrike Cope	Bojangles' Ford
4	3	Kyle Petty	Mello Yello Pontiac	21	26	Brett Bodine	Quaker State Ford
5	2	Ricky Rudd	Tide Chevrolet	22	32	Bobby Hillin	Heilig-Meyers Ford
6	5	Harry Gant	Skoal Bandit Chevrolet	23	25	Todd Bodine	Factory Stores Ford
7	4	Terry Labonte	Kellogg's Chevrolet	24	31	John Andretti	Tex Racing Chevrolet
8	13	Rick Mast	Skoal Classic Ford	25	33	Jeff Purvis	Kodak Film Chevrolet
9	24	Dale Jarrett	Interstate Batteries Chevrolet	26	30	Jay Hedgecock	Wilson-Inman Ford
10	12	Ken Schrader	Kodiak Chevrolet	27	22	Kenny Wallace	Dirt Devil Pontiac
11	7	Darrell Waltrip	Western Auto Chevrolet	28	14	Hut Stricklin	McDonald's Ford
12	20	Bobby Labonte	Maxwell House Ford	29	18	Ted Musgrave	Jasper Engines Ford
13	17	Jimmy Spencer	Meineke Mufflers Ford	30	15	Dick Trickle	Manheim Auctions Chevrolet
14	28	Michael Waltrip	Pennzoil Pontiac	31	23	Geoff Bodine	Carolina Opry Ford
15	29	Wally Dallenbach	Keystone Beer Ford	32	21	Morgan Shepherd	Citgo Ford
16	6	Mark Martin	Valvoline Ford	33	34	Rick Wilson	STP Pontiac
17	19	Lake Speed	Motorcraft Ford	34	16	Jeff Gordon	DuPont Auto Finishes Chevrolet

MELLO YELLO 500

Rookie sensation Jeff Gordon races wheel to wheel with Dale Earnhardt. Earnhardt finished the day in third place.

The championship hunt had certainly heated up, and both Dale Earnhardt and Rusty Wallace had reasons to be congratulated when the teams unloaded in the Charlotte garage area.

Wallace's victory at North Wilkesboro was his eighth of the season, and when combined with Kyle Petty's June Pocono victory, it gave the Pontiac troops a modern-era (since 1972 when the schedule was reduced to approximately 30 races per year) record nine wins. It was the highest number of Pontiac victories in a single season since 1962, when the marquee won 21 of 53 in 1962.

Earnhardt spent all day Thursday being feted by his hometown of Kannapolis, with "Dale Earnhardt Boulevard" named in his honor. His

Team owner Richard Childress keeps a sharp eye on the track watching his own car as well as the Pontiac of Rusty Wallace.

Everything is quiet at dawn around the speedway. Crews slowly begin preparations for the Mello Yello 500 at Charlotte.

friends and family shared the pleasure that came from his recognition by the city fathers where he grew up and where his mother still lives on Sedan Street. Profits from the day went to the city's school system to improve education of Kannapolis' youth.

When the seven-week, seven-race string began at Bristol, Wallace had trailed by 324 points and Dale had appeared to be a lock for the title. Many thought he would have enough points by Charlotte to clinch the title in front of his hometown crowd. But, instead, Wallace had chopped, hacked, clawed and ground the point lead down to 72 as Charlotte approached.

The Mello Yello 500 was a new adventure for most of the teams after NASCAR installed the "5-5-51" rules for car configuration for the Charlotte race. The height of the front air-dam was raised from 3.5 to five inches. The rear spoiler height was lowered from six inches to five, with spoiler

square inches reduced accordingly. And car roof heights were raised one-half inch to 51 inches. All the changes were mandated to slow the cars slightly and create a better safety situation for drivers.

Teams had been given the rules in plenty of time, and drivers had used the pre-event track testing time to help dial in the handling characteristics of their machines to the new specs. Some teams, like Wallace's, had taken their cars to the wind tunnel to find ways to help balance the downforce on the cars within the new rule framework.

During the six weeks prior to Charlotte, the contenders for the championship had all fallen by the wayside. The closest anyone was to Wallace was Dale Jarrett, who was 306 behind Earnhardt and 234 behind Rusty. Mark Martin was 350 behind Earnhardt, with fifth-place Morgan Shepherd 523 behind.

It would be a shoot-out between the two drivers — much like the battle in 1989 where Wallace came from behind to beat Earnhardt.

Prior to the race, the two friends spoke of their pleasure to be racing for the title between themselves and their two teams. They felt that each driver brought out the best in the other — and that the teams were highly competitive, as well. Neither could be more delighted, they confessed, than to have the pleasure of beating the other for the 1993 NASCAR Winston Cup.

While Wallace and Earnhardt were doing their "Mutual Admiration" press conference, Robert Yates and his team were preparing a blitzkrieg. Little did any team in the garage area know what Larry McReynolds and the Havoline team were about to spring on them come Sunday.

After Winston Pole Night was over, Jeff Gordon had shocked the entire assemblage by turning the fastest qualifying lap. He joined Bobby Labonte as rookies notching pole positions during the 1993 season, and car-owner Rick Hendrick couldn't have been happier. The auto magnate hoped it would carry through on Sunday, because a Chevrolet win would help the Bowtie Brigade in their quest for the Manufacturer's Championship. The points had tightened even more with Rusty's North Wilkesboro win, and now Chevrolet led Ford and Pontiac 169-164-161.

For the fifth-straight race, Irvan had the Havoline Ford on the front row, and Geoff Bodine and Ken Schrader locked up the third and fourth starting positions. Bill Elliott and a surprising Greg Sacks were the third row, with Martin and Ricky Rudd making up the fourth row. Earnhardt and Brett Bodine completed the top ten. One of the other surprises of qualifying was the 11th-fastest time turned by Joe Nemechek, who replaced Jeff

Purvis in the Kodak Chevrolet.

Hooters Restaurants used the Charlotte race to announce that the company would return to NASCAR Winston Cup racing in 1994 as the primary sponsor for Loy Allen, Jr. And Gary Bechtel's Diamond Ridge Racing would be another new team entering the Winston Cup wars in 1994, with NASCAR Busch Grand National championship contender Steve Grissom as the driver. Harry Gant confirmed he would retire following the 1994 season, from Leo Jackson's Skoal Chevrolet team.

After the "Humpyland Hoopla" pre-race activities (including a ramp-jumping garbage truck!) were over, the green flag dropped — and it wasn't long before some of the competitors were hoping that Irvan would collide with the dumpster! That might slow him down!

Ernie just flat drove away — and took the entire field out behind the woodshed for an old-fashioned butt-whipping. He led for 328 of the 334 laps, set a new race average speed and was brought back in check only by a late caution for oil on the track.

When the second (and final) yellow came out on lap 307, Irvan was more than 14 seconds ahead of the field and cruising.

The yellow gave the few remaining cars on the lead lap a chance to see what the rear of the Havo-

Ernie Irvan was the dominant car all day long. Irvan held off a late challenge from Mark Martin for the victory.

193

Jeff Gordon began the race from the pole position; however, he managed to lead only one lap, the 64th.

line Ford looked like, but when the green flew for the final time on lap 313, Irvan merely dropped the hammer and motored away again.

The only car with a hope to beat him was Martin, but Mark had nothing for the black Ford and had his hands full with a determined Earnhardt, running third behind the Valvoline machine.

Irvan's winning margin was 1.83 seconds, with Martin able to handle Earnhardt and finish second. Right behind Earnhardt was Wallace, who lost ten points to Dale in the point race after Earnhardt led, but Rusty didn't. The DuPont Flash completed his strong showing to claim fifth, ahead of Jimmy Spencer and Kyle Petty, the final driver on the lead lap. Rudd was a single lap down in eighth place, while Schrader beat Elliott for ninth place in their battle for supremacy in the two-laps-behind category.

Victory Lane was an emotional roller-coaster

for Irvan and the Robert Yates team. Irvan had finally won at what he considers his "home" track — the same place where eight years ago he had worked as a laborer, welding seats while racing on the dirt Concord Speedway just a few miles away.

For Robert Yates and his wife Carolyn, however, the Charlotte race had been a difficult one. Charlotte police officer John Burnette and his partner, Anthony Nobles, had been murdered while trying to apprehend a suspect earlier in the week. Burnette was a long-time friend of Yates' son and Havoline crew member Doug. The Burnette and Yates families had been close for years. After Irvan's victory, Yates and his wife said they would donate $50,000 of the team's winnings to the Charlotte Police Benevolent Association in memory of the two officers.

"Everyone has said that we've been heroes since we lost Davey," Robert said of his decision to donate the money. "Police officers like these two young men are the real heroes. I'm just glad we can do something to help them, as others have helped us this year."

Ernie Irvan is all smiles after taking the Robert Yates team back to victory lane in Charlotte.

Fin. Pos.	Str. Pos.	Driver	Team	Fin. Pos.	Str. Pos.	Driver	Team
1	2	Ernie Irvan	Havoline Ford	22	27	Dick Trickle	Manheim Auctions Chevrolet
2	7	Mark Martin	Valvoline Ford	23	23	Hut Stricklin	McDonald's Ford
3	9	Dale Earnhardt	GM Goodwrench Chevrolet	24	33	Wally Dallenbach	Keystone Beer Ford
4	21	Rusty Wallace	Miller Genuine Draft Pontiac	25	11	Joe Nemechek	Kodak Film Chevrolet
5	1	Jeff Gordon	DuPont Auto Finishes Chevrolet	26	38	Dale Jarrett	Interstate Batteries Chevrolet
6	15	Jimmy Spencer	Meineke Mufflers Ford	27	20	Michael Waltrip	Pennzoil Pontiac
7	31	Kyle Petty	Mello Yello Pontiac	28	41	Bobby Labonte	Maxwell House Ford
8	8	Ricky Rudd	Tide Chevrolet	29	30	Jeremy Mayfield	Mac Tools Ford
9	4	Ken Schrader	Kodiak Chevrolet	30	35	Mike Wallace	Duron Paints Ford
10	5	Bill Elliott	Budweiser Ford	31	40	John Andretti	Tex Racing Chevrolet
11	36	Lake Speed	Motorcraft Ford	32	6	Greg Sacks	Country Time Ford
12	13	Harry Gant	Skoal Bandit Chevrolet	33	39	Chad Little	Kleenex Ford
13	3	Geoff Bodine	Family Channel Ford	34	32	Jerry O'Neil	O'Neil Racing Chevrolet
14	16	Morgan Shepherd	Citgo Ford	35	42	Kenny Wallace	Dirt Devil Pontiac
15	10	Brett Bodine	Quaker State Ford	36	18	Rick Wilson	STP Pontiac
16	22	Terry Labonte	Kellogg's Chevrolet	37	28	Bobby Hamilton	Fina Lube Ford
17	34	Sterling Marlin	Raybestos Brakes Ford	38	29	Jim Sauter	Burger King Ford
18	12	Rick Mast	Skoal Classic Ford	39	14	Derrike Cope	Bojangles Ford
19	24	Darrell Waltrip	Western Auto Chevrolet	40	19	Rich Bickle	Kraft Bullseye Ford
20	37	Bobby Hillin	Heilig-Meyers Ford	41	25	Andy Hillenburg	Diamond Ridge Racing Chevrolet
21	26	Ted Musgrave	Jasper Engines Ford	42	17	Todd Bodine	Factory Stores Ford

AC DELCO 500

NORTH CAROLINA MOTOR SPEEDWAY

OCTOBER 24, 1993

Bill Elliott and Mark Martin take off in pursuit of Ernie Irvan.

With just three races remaining, a confident Rusty Wallace cruised into Frank Wilson's North Carolina Motor Speedway feeling "the need for speed." Wallace had run away from the field to win the spring race here Rusty was happy to be back in his familiar "Midnight" Miller Pontiac at The Rock.

Still smarting from the spanking administered at Charlotte by Ernie Irvan, teams spent little time with horseplay and joking at Rockingham. A gritty feeling of determination permeated the garage area with every team dedicated to showing that Irvan's dominant Charlotte win was a one-time performance.

Wallace knew time was growing short for his championship bid. Sure, he had chopped Dale Earnhardt's point lead down to a manageable size, but the Miller driver had been on a tear that everyone knew could not last forever. In the last seven races, he had finished lower than third just once — and that was his fourth the last time out at CMS. He had notched three victories in those seven races and had been second twice.

Rusty Wallace enjoys a victory kiss from one of the Unocal Racestoppers.

Mark Martin and Ken Schrader started from the pole but neither could handle Rusty Wallace in the end.

But he hadn't been able to get close enough to Earnhardt to make the black Chevrolet driver break a sweat. If Wallace really was to turn the heat up, he needed a victory here at Rockingham.

Earnhardt, on the other hand, had raced hard throughout the seven events, and had suffered a little bad luck in two of the events that allowed Wallace to close to within striking distance. But Dale felt the pressure was on Wallace to continue his hot streak. He had just as much confidence in his own equipment as Wallace did, and Earnhardt knew his combat-tested team would answer any challenge Wallace could throw at them.

Both teams were ready for Rockingham. They knew there would be other teams who would factor into the race results, but the title challengers had it all together for the 492-lap race.

Mark Martin showed he and the Valvoline team were ready, with Martin putting a four-year-old Roush Racing chassis on the pole and drawing within one pole position of Ken Schrader for the

$40,000 Busch year-end bonus to the driver with the most poles in a season.

Schrader, hoping to lock up the award, failed by .02 seconds and took the other front row starting slot with his Kodiak Chevrolet. Irvan continued his tear since slotting into the Havoline Ford, qualifying third-fastest — the first time he had been off the front row since Richmond. Bill Elliott notched his second-straight top-five qualifying position to sit outside Irvan, with the third row made up of Ricky Rudd and Kyle Petty. The DuPont Flash was seventh-fastest, with steady Morgan Shepherd eighth-fastest in the Citgo Ford.

Rounding out the top-10 were Harry Gant and Dick Trickle, giving the Manheim Auctions Chevrolet its first top-10 start of the season.

Where were the championship contenders? Both struggled in qualifying, with Wallace making it into the first-round with the 18th-fastest time, and Earnhardt moving to 22nd on the basis of second-round qualifying, earning his way onto the frontstretch to avoid pitting on the backstretch all day.

It was announced that while teams were making final preparations, Jimmy Hensley would be the driver for the next three years of the "55" car fielded by RaDiUs Racing, replacing Ted Musgrave. Hensley was not in a car for the Rockingham race but would finish out the season driving the Kodak Chevrolet for Morgan-McClure Racing at Phoenix and Atlanta.

After the early laps in the race sorted out, first Jimmy Spencer and then Gant appeared ready to end their long winless droughts. Spencer's bid ended with a rounded-off lug nut during a pit stop, dropping him from contention. Gant's performance at the front of the field was curtailed by a set of tires that didn't respond to his wishes, and he later broke a valve spring.

While those two were at the front of the field, Earnhardt was struggling — and

Wallace's team worked steadily through the first half of the event to get his Miller Pontiac handling better.

The handling on the Goodwrench Chevrolet just wasn't there, and Earnhardt manhandled the car around the tricky Rockingham track.

Wallace, on the other hand, finally got the

Bobby Hillin and John Andretti take evasive action to miss a spinning Greg Sacks.

The crew of the Miller Genuine Draft Pontiac deserve a lot of credit for putting Rusty Wallace in the thick of the championship battle.

199

Pontiac to his liking, and went to the front on the 312th lap. He would lead the remainder of the race, except for a couple of laps during green-flag stops and did all he could to gain on Earnhardt by posting his ninth victory of the season and leading the most laps. Rusty's point total for the race was 185 at the end — maximum points.

But Wallace's victory wasn't the most joyous he posted during the year. Right in his mirror was Earnhardt, who had closed to less than two seconds behind the Pontiac with just ten laps to go. Just when it looked like Earnhardt was going to move onto Wallace's bumper for a ten-lap shootout, his right front tire started leaking air — and Earnhardt was forced to back off and begin fighting Elliott for the runner-up slot.

Earnhardt maintained his position, Elliott was forced to finish third, and after 500 miles and more than 4.5 hours of battle, Wallace had won, but gained just ten points on Earnhardt.

The frustration was beginning to show a bit in Rusty. He had been on a blistering run during the last eight races, but he was still 72 points behind Earnhardt, and there were just two races left to go.

Earnhardt was parrying every Wallace thrust. Wallace's fierce determination to win the 1993 NASCAR Winston Cup Championship was blunted at every turn by Earnhardt's valiant efforts not to lose the title at this stage of the season.

The cross-country trip to the Arizona desert faced truck drivers. Practice would begin in Phoenix in just five days.

T.W. Taylor struggles to get the Children's Miracle Network Ford back in the right direction.

UNOCAL PIT CREW CHAMPS

Throughout the year, the unsung heroes of the NASCAR Winston Cup Series are the team members who do the car preparation and then jump over the wall, servicing the race cars during pit stops.

At Rockingham each year, the pit crews have their own chance to shine, taking center stage in Unocal's annual Pit Crew Competition. Not only are pride and bragging rights at stake, but Unocal also posts a payoff for the top 10 teams. The winners get to split $8,600, with the second-quickest team receiving $4,100.

All through 1993, the fastest team on pit road has consistently been the Miller Pontiac group headed by Buddy Parrott. At times, however, other teams had bested the Miller crew and the October shoot-out at Rockingham would prove the ultimate test by which teams would measure themselves.

A total of 31 teams entered the competition, and when it was over, Parrott and his group had proven what they had done all year was no fluke. They set a new world record of 22.454 seconds, breaking the mark set in 1991 by Bud Moore's team by more than a tenth of a second.

Donnie Richeson, in charge of Brett Bodine's team, finished second, nearly a second behind the winners, with Steve Hmiel's Mark Martin team finishing third. Mike Hill (Hut Stricklin) and the McDonald's team was fourth-fastest, while Doug Hewitt (Michael Waltrip) and the Pennzoil Pontiac crew claimed fifth place.

Fin. Pos.	Str. Pos.	Driver	Team	Fin. Pos.	Str. Pos.	Driver	Team
1	18	Rusty Wallace	Miller Draft Pontiac	22	12	Bobby Labonte	Maxwell House Ford
2	22	Dale Earnhardt	GM Goodwrench Chevrolet	23	14	Joe Nemechek	Kodak Film Chevrolet
3	4	Bill Elliott	Budweiser Ford	24	20	Hut Stricklin	McDonald's Ford
4	9	Harry Gant	Skoal Bandit Chevrolet	25	23	Todd Bodine	Factory Stores Ford
5	1	Mark Martin	Valvoline Ford	26	28	Rick Wilson	STP Pontiac
6	3	Ernie Irvan	Havoline Ford	27	34	Dave Marcis	Style Auto Chevrolet
7	16	Darrell Waltrip	Western Auto Chevrolet	28	32	Ted Musgrave	Jasper Engines Ford
8	2	Ken Schrader	Kodiak Chevrolet	29	37	Jimmy Means	Means Racing Ford
9	10	Dick Trickle	Manheim Auctions Chevrolet	30	21	Dale Jarrett	Interstate Batteries Chevrolet
10	19	Geoff Bodine	Family Channel Ford	31	30	Wally Dallenbach	Keystone Beer Ford
11	8	Morgan Shepherd	Citgo Ford	32	27	Greg Sacks	Country Time Ford
12	25	Sterling Marlin	Raybestos Brakes Ford	33	38	Bobby Hillin	Heilig-Meyers Ford
13	6	Kyle Petty	Mello Yello Pontiac	34	35	Jimmy Horton	Active Racing Chevrolet
14	5	Ricky Rudd	Tide Chevrolet	35	11	Brett Bodine	Quaker State Ford
15	24	Terry Labonte	Kellogg's Chevrolet	36	33	Mike Wallace	FDP Brakes Ford
16	31	Lake Speed	Motorcraft Ford	37	41	Kenny Wallace	Dirt Devil Pontiac
17	13	Rick Mast	Skoal Classic Ford	38	40	Jerry Hill	Bell Motors Chevrolet
18	29	Michael Waltrip	Pennzoil Pontiac	39	39	John Andretti	Tex Racing Chevrolet
19	17	Derrike Cope	Bojangles' Ford	40	26	T.W. Taylor	Childrens' Miracle Network Ford
20	15	Jimmy Spencer	Meineke Mufflers Ford	41	36	Loy Allen	Naturally Fresh Ford
21	7	Jeff Gordon	DuPont Auto Finishes Chevrolet				

SLICK 50 500

R. J. Reynolds made a huge announcement at Phoenix: Hut Stricklin would be driving the Smokin' Joe Ford in '94.

*I*n just five days, the scene had shifted from the lush, piney Sandhills of North Carolina to the arid Arizona desert in the Valley of the Sun. In years past, the NASCAR Winston Cup Series visit has been held under the broiling sun normally associated with the desert.

This year, however, the weekend at Buddy Jobe's flat one-mile track was among the most pleasant in the race's six-year history. Highs were in the low '80s — much the same as the weather back in the Southeast. Nights were warm — in the low 70s, and team members stole a few hours to see some of the area attractions — ranging from the Grand Canyon three hours north of Phoenix, to Las Vegas, just a hop, skip and a cheap airline ticket away. Great (and scenic) restaurants abound in Phoenix, and although some drivers thought that because they were in the Southwest they could slide in and out unrecognized for a quiet dinner, they quickly found out differently. There were plenty of fans to recognize them.

Mark Martin can't hide this grin as he celebrates his win in Phoenix.

1993
NASCAR Winston Cup Series
Slick-50 500

CHAMPION

Phoenix International Raceway
October 31, 1993

The Raybestos Ford gets sideways, and Ernie Irvan has to go high to avoid contact.

Phoenix had sold tickets to residents of more than 40 states and hotel rooms were filled. More than 90,000 NASCAR race fans swelled the one-mile track to the near-bursting point, prompting Jobe to schedule the addition of 7,000 seats in time for next year's race.

There was plenty going on in Phoenix — and competition for the recreational dollar was at a premium. How's this for some pickings: NFL Phoenix Cardinals vs. New Orleans Saints (Sunday afternoon). NBA Phoenix Suns vs. New York Knicks (Friday night). Michael Carbajal vs. Domingo Sosa IBF/WBC Junior Flyweight title bout (Saturday night). Arizona State vs. University of Washington Pac-10 football (Saturday). Arizona State Fair all week. Vince Gill in concert at the State Fair Saturday night!

Head-to-head, against all comers, Phoenix International Raceway's sold-out crowd outnumbered everyone. In fact, the race crowd was bigger than the combined ASU/Washington and NFL Cardinals/Saints attendance!

Who says they don't love their NASCAR racing in the desert!

While almost everyone else was enjoying a few days in the Phoenix area before the race, Dale Earnhardt had a "mini-vacation" of his own. Immediately following Rockingham, he headed for New Mexico, where he spent two days hunting in 10,000-foot-high mountains. On the second day he bagged a trophy elk and then headed for the Valley of the Sun to protect his scant 72-point lead over Rusty Wallace.

Wallace admitted before the race that he needed a little more help from Lady Luck. She had been his steady companion over the last several races, and he needed her company for just two more races if he was to win his second NASCAR Winston Cup.

With just two races to go, the title was within easy reach of Earnhardt. For Wallace to win the championship, Dale would have to stumble either here or at Atlanta — and Rusty would need to be near-perfect in both races.

After Bill Elliott notched his second pole position of the season, and Dick Trickle responded with an outstanding run to claim the outside of the front row with his Manheim Chevrolet, the folks in Kenny Schrader's garage stall danced with delight. Schrader had six pole positions for the season and Mark Martin had five. Now, with only one race left, the most Martin could do would be to tie Schrader with six poles by winning at Atlanta — and the tie-breaker for the $40,000 Busch bonus for most poles was the number of outside poles. Schrader had two — and Martin only one. With help from Elliott and Trickle, Kenny had locked the Busch bucks.

Martin qualified third, with Ricky Rudd outside him. Ernie Irvan and Wallace made up the third row, with Sterling Marlin and Schrader in the fourth row. Jeff Gordon and Chuck Bown, driving the Pedigree Chevrolet, completed the top-ten. Earnhardt would start 11th.

After R.J. Reynolds announced its Camel sponsorship of the "Smokin' Joe's Racing" team of Travis Carter and Hut Stricklin for the coming season, Junior Johnson confirmed that Jimmy Spencer would move to the McDonald's team for 1994. Country Time Lemonade told the world it would back a six-race effort in 1994 with Neil

Bonnett behind the wheel of the Phoenix Racing Chevrolets, powered by Richard Childress engines. The Gary Bechtal-owned Diamond Ridge team, announced just two races ago at Charlotte, made its debut with Steve Grissom behind the wheel, while Loy Allen, Jr. was in the Tri-Star Motorsports Ford instead of Greg Sacks.

Obviously, there was plenty to keep the media folk busy this weekend!

The last time Kyle Petty had ridden his Harley any distance to a race, he won at Pocono. When he announced plans to ride his Hog to Phoenix, Harry Gant was the first to ask Kyle if he needed any company. Harry's memory is still good — and he was willing to try just about anything to get back in the win column, especially after his disappointment at Rockingham. Along with some others, Kyle and Harry rode off into the sunset Monday — and arrived at Phoenix a little saddle-weary Wednesday afternoon.

After all the preparation, it was finally time to race, and after Dick Trickle led a few, Martin blew past the yellow Chevrolet — and began to handle

A crew member for Rusty Wallace stretches all the way across the MGD Pontiac to clear the windshield.

the newly-paved oval the same way Irvan had handled Charlotte two races prior.

Mark was dialed in — and he admitted after he cruised to his fifth victory of the year that he had been a little lucky because his team had not been able to find the right handle for his Valvoline Ford during sunny Friday and Saturday practice sessions.

But Sunday's weather was unusually overcast, with temperatures in the 70s — and the Ford responded with a performance that was good enough to lead more than 80 percent of the 312 laps.

and Michael Waltrip came home ninth with his Pennzoil Pontiac. Rick Mast finished 10th.

Where was Wallace?

His title dreams took a major lick when he cut a tire on lap 191. He was running fourth at the time and looked like he had plenty of car to finish within the top four. Earnhardt, at the time, was running around tenth, trying to get his Chevrolet to handle.

Wallace headed for the pits, trailing a shower of sparks. The sway bar was dragging on the asphalt, and by the time he reached pit road, his crew had to replace the sway bar. During the next

Incidental contact from Dale Earnhardt brought Ken Schrader's day to an early close.

In the final stages of the race, Irvan made a run at Martin but came up short and had to settle for second. Kyle had an outstanding day, moving from his 27th starting position to finish third, while Earnhardt all but locked up his sixth Winston Cup with a steady fourth place. Pole-sitter Elliott came home fifth, with Rudd sixth and Darrell Waltrip seventh. Rookie Bobby Labonte posted another top-10 finish with his eighth-place finish

yellow they made repairs, but it was too late. When they were finished, Rusty was two laps in arrears, and in the remaining few yellows, he could not get himself into position to try to get either of the laps back.

As the desert sun set, Kyle had biked to his best finish since his Pocono victory. He was last seen calling the NASCAR Advantage road service for maps to ride his Harley to EVERY 1994 race!

Martin had returned to the August form that saw him record four straight victories. His trip home from the desert was a pleasant one.

For Wallace, the battle was nearly over. He refused to admit defeat, planning an all-out assault on Atlanta. But he was realistic, as well. He knew that 126 points would be nearly impossible to overcome in a single race.

For Earnhardt, the long quest was almost completed. Only a single race stood in his way of a sixth title. He had bagged his trophy elk during the first part of his hunting trip. He had nearly captured the title in the second half of the week. He now needed to finish only 34th or higher at Atlanta.

The mountains in the region provide a beautiful backdrop for the Slick 50 500 at Phoenix.

Fin. Pos.	Str. Pos.	Driver	Team	Fin. Pos.	Str. Pos.	Driver	Team
1	3	Mark Martin	Valvoline Ford	23	31	Derrike Cope	Bojangles' Ford
2	5	Ernie Irvan	Havoline Ford	24	10	Chuck Bown	Pedigree Food Chevrolet
3	27	Kyle Petty	Mello Yello Pontiac	25	30	Todd Bodine	Factory Stores Ford
4	11	Dale Earnhardt	GM Goodwrench Chevrolet	26	40	Loy Allen	Country Time Ford
5	1	Bill Elliott	Budweiser Ford	27	17	Jimmy Spencer	Meineke Mufflers Ford
6	4	Ricky Rudd	Tide Chevrolet	28	12	Brett Bodine	Quaker State Ford
7	21	Darrell Waltrip	Western Auto Chevrolet	29	18	Steve Grissom	Diamond Ridge Chevrolet
8	20	Bobby Labonte	Maxwell House Ford	30	7	Sterling Marlin	Raybestos Brakes Ford
9	23	Michael Waltrip	Pennzoil Pontiac	31	2	Dick Trickle	Manheim Auctions Chevrolet
10	13	Rick Mast	Skoal Classic Ford	32	29	Jimmy Hensley	Kodak Film Chevrolet
11	22	Morgan Shepherd	Citgo Ford	33	8	Ken Schrader	Kodiak Chevrolet
12	15	Harry Gant	Skoal Bandit Chevrolet	34	35	Wally Dallenbach	Keystone Beer Ford
13	16	Lake Speed	Motorcraft Ford	35	9	Jeff Gordon	DuPont Auto Finishes Chevrolet
14	26	Terry Labonte	Kellogg's Chevrolet	36	28	Hut Stricklin	McDonald's Ford
15	36	Ted Musgrave	Jasper Engines Ford	37	41	Terry Fisher	Exide Batteries Pontiac
16	14	Dale Jarrett	Interstate Batteries Chevrolet	38	39	Rich Woodland	National Cold Storage Oldsmobile
17	32	Kenny Wallace	Dirt Devil Pontiac	39	38	Mike Chase	Star Race Computers Chevrolet
18	35	Bobby Hillin	Heilig-Meyers Ford	40	34	John Andretti	Hagan Racing Chevrolet
19	6	Rusty Wallace	Miller Genuine Draft Pontiac	41	43	Wayne Jacks	Imperial Palace Hotel Pontiac
20	37	Rick Wilson	STP Pontiac	42	42	Dirk Stephens	Mark's Drywall Ford
21	25	Rick Carelli	Chesrown Auto Group Chevrolet	43	19	Geoff Bodine	Family Channel Ford
22	24	Ron Hornaday	Spears Manufacturing Chevrolet				

HOOTERS 500

With a massive crowd looking on, the field comes into the pits for service.

*I*n the days prior to the 500-miler at Atlanta Motor Speedway, Dale Earnhardt's team was busy in the shop at Welcome, NC, making his Goodwrench Chevrolet and its back-up as identical—and bullet-proof—as possible.

Earnhardt and his team knew that all he had to do was finish 34th or better to end a successful quest for the NASCAR Winston Cup. With attrition expected at the 1.5-mile oval, Dale needed to avoid trouble—and be able to run for the duration of the 328 laps. If he could do that, he would be the man on the stage at the Waldorf.

For Rusty Wallace, however, the task that lay ahead had become one of gargantuan proportions. He was faced with having to win the race and lead the most laps if he were to have any chance of catching Earnhardt.

In addition, Wallace was at the mercy of the racing gods. He was totally dependent on Earnhardt suffering some problem or another and being forced from the race in its early stages. He needed both sides of

Rusty Wallace did all he could do to catch Dale Earnhardt

for the NASCAR Winston Cup Championship.

Rusty won the battle, Dale won the war.

the equation to be there if he were to win his second title.

Harry Gant surprised everyone in qualifying, winning his first pole of the season and nipping Brett Bodine in the process. Rick Mast, who runs extremely well at Charlotte and Atlanta, lined up right behind his Skoal mate by qualifying third, with Ted Musgrave posting his best qualifying run of the year to take fourth.

Jimmy Spencer, like Musgrave, making his final start for this team, qualified fifth, and Bobby Hamilton gave qualifying a jolt, putting his Fina Ford, owned by Dick Moroso, sixth on the grid. Ernie Irvan and hometown favorite Bill Elliott made up fourth row, while Rich Bickle continued the qualifying surprises by posting the ninth-fastest lap. Lake Speed completed the top-10 qualifiers.

Where were the championship combatants?

Right where they could see each other, side-by-side in the tenth row. Earnhardt had qualified 19th in his back-up car, while Wallace made the

cut in first-round qualifying by notching the 20th-quickest lap.

There was plenty to talk about during the Atlanta weekend other than the championship. Jack Roush announced The Family Channel would sponsor Ted Musgrave's Ford in 1994, and Lake Speed and Bud Moore unveiled the new Ford Quality Care colors for the next season a race early. Hoosier Tires announced its return to Winston Cup competition in 1994. Ricky Rudd unveiled his Tide Ford for the coming season, complete with car number 10. Cale Yarborough and Derrike Cope unveiled the Fingerhut Ford they will campaign during 1994. And D.K. Ulrich announced a new team for next season, with USAir and Jasper Engines as sponsors and Greg Sacks driving. The car will carry "77"—and the RaDiUs team, carrying number 55, will continue next season with Jimmy Hensley as the driver, but with a new sponsor.

But the focus of the largest crowd ever to see a sporting event in the state of Georgia was riveted

Number one & Number two. Then great competitors battle it out in Atlanta.

Ernie Irvan came back from this incident for a respectable second place finish.

on the Earnhardt/Wallace struggle when the green flag fell.

Early in the race, Gant appeared ready to win his first event of the year, but he was trapped a lap down when he pitted under green and a yellow ensued. Fight as he would, Gant never was a factor after that. His day ended after a scrape with the wall.

Wallace had moved through the field and became the dominant car for the remainder of the race. He would lead nine times for 189 laps, doing everything he could to wrest the Cup from Earnhardt.

But at the 150-lap mark, attrition had ended his chances. When Neil Bonnett went to the garage, Brett Bodine and Bobby Hillin tangled, ending the day for each. Jimmy Horton was involved in a wreck that ended the day for Geoff Bodine and sent Ken Schrader and Jimmy Spencer limping around the track the rest of the race.

When Rick Mast blew up and Rick Carelli's day ended, Earnhardt was one car away from his title. It came just a few laps later when T.W. Taylor lost a battle with the Atlanta wall.

Wallace's tenth trip to victory lane wasn't assured quite yet, however. He had to survive a charge from Earnhardt that ended with Dale slapping into Greg Sacks, ruining the aerodynamics of his Chevrolet. And then, with the laps winding down, Wallace was forced to punish his Goodyear Eagles to catch and pass Darrell Waltrip.

Waltrip's only chance for victory came via

mileage—and he tried to stretch the last 78 laps into his first win of the season. After a quick stop for fuel with just 17 laps left, Rusty put the hammer down—and managed to get past Darrell with four laps to go. On the final lap around the track, Waltrip ran out—and was forced to watch Ricky Rudd pass him to take second place.

Darrell was third, with Bill Elliott the leading Ford at the end of the race, in fourth place.

Rudd, leaving to join the Ford forces for 1994 with his own team, ironically, was the hero for Chevrolet. The Manufacturer's title was on the line at Atlanta, with Chevrolet and Ford a point apart. Whichever make finished ahead of the other would win the title. Rudd clinched the crown for the Bowtie Brigade with his second place. Chevrolet's winning margin was just a single point.

The battle for point positions further back in

the field saw Kyle Petty move ahead of Morgan Shepherd for fifth place in the standings. Shepherd's engine failed—and it dropped him to seventh in the final standings. Ernie Irvan climbed to sixth.

Elliott's fourth place helped him up a notch in the final standings to eighth place, with Kenny Schrader falling to ninth. Rudd claimed the final position on the stage at the Waldorf with his tenth-place finish in the final standings.

Wallace celebrated his tenth victory of the season with a backwards lap in honor of Alan Kulwicki, and carried a flag with a "28" on it for Davey Allison. He started his lap, and heard a noise behind him. He looked—and there was Earnhardt, also headed on a "Polish Victory Lap" and carrying a flag with an orange "7" and a tomato-red "28."

The two friends, who had fought each other hammer and tongs for this year's title, made their way around the track side-by-side in honor of their fallen competitors.

The final margin was 80 points in the season-long battle, and Earnhardt had earned the right to sit at the head table at the Waldorf Astoria once again.

His quest was ended. The disappointment of the 1992 season had been avenged. He had won his sixth championship, and now stood ready to challenge Richard Petty's record of seven Winston Cups.

Now, as he headed for the farm outside his native Kannapolis, he could begin his winter preparations. First was a little hunting trip with buddy Neil Bonnett. Then, the Championship week in New York. And then it would be time to focus on the race he most wants to win—the 1994 Daytona 500.

... *"No one appreciates the fans and the way they have supported our Goodwrench team more than Richard Childress and myself."*

Dale Earnhardt

Harry Gant, a favorite of race fans everywhere will make 1994 his last season.

Outstanding pit work enabled Dale Earnhardt to run near the top all year long, en route to his sixth NASCAR Winston Cup Championship.

Fin. Pos.	Str. Pos.	Driver	Team	Fin. Pos.	Str. Pos.	Driver	Team
1	20	Rusty Wallace	Miller Genuine Draft Pontiac	22	42	Hut Stricklin	McDonald's Ford
2	13	Ricky Rudd	Tide Chevrolet	23	36	Rick Wilson	STP Pontiac
3	28	Darrell Waltrip	Western Auto Chevrolet	24	26	Greg Sacks	Country Time Ford
4	8	Bill Elliott	Budweiser Ford	25	17	Jimmy Hensley	Kodak Film Chevrolet
5	18	Dick Trickle	Manheim Auctions Chevrolet	26	10	Lake Speed	Motorcraft Ford
6	31	Michael Waltrip	Pennzoil Pontiac	27	21	Ken Schrader	Kodiak Chevrolet
7	29	Dale Jarrett	Interstate Batteries Chevrolet	28	1	Harry Gant	Skoal Bandit Chevrolet
8	4	Ted Musgrave	Jasper Engines Ford	29	24	Loy Allen	Naturally Fresh Foods Ford
9	22	Phil Parsons	Factory Stores Ford	30	40	Kenny Wallace	Dirt Devil Pontiac
10	19	Dale Earnhardt	GM Goodwrench Chevrolet	31	15	Jeff Gordon	DuPont Auto Finishes Chevrolet
11	41	Kyle Petty	Mello Yello Pontiac	32	16	Morgan Shepherd	Citgo Ford
12	7	Ernie Irvan	Havoline Ford	33	38	Wally Dallenbach	Keystone Beer Ford
13	30	Terry Labonte	Kellogg's Chevrolet	34	39	T. W. Taylor	Childrens' Miracle Network Ford
14	32	Bobby Labonte	Maxwell House Ford	35	25	Rick Carelli	Total Petroleum Chevrolet
15	23	Mike Wallace	Duron Paints Pontiac	36	9	Rich Bickle	Bull's-Eye Ford
16	5	Jimmy Spencer	Meineke Mufflers Ford	37	3	Rick Mast	Skoal Classic
17	34	Sterling Marlin	Raybestos Brakes Ford	38	14	Jimmy Horton	Wheels Race Cards Chevrolet
18	37	Dave Marcis	Fresh Express Chevrolet	39	11	Geoff Bodine	Family Channel Ford
19	27	Derrike Cope	Bojangles' Ford	40	2	Brett Bodine	Quaker State Ford
20	33	Mark Martin	Valvoline Ford	41	12	Bobby Hillin	Heilig-Meyers Ford
21	6	Bobby Hamilton	Fina Lube Ford	42	35	Neil Bonnett	Western Steer Chevrolet

Wired for sight and sound, the gas man for Ricky Rudd's Tide Chevrolet is set to go.

REMEMBERING
1993

The whole Bodine family will be in Daytona ready to make another charge for the NASCAR Winston Cup title.

Two rising stars of NASCAR, Jeff Gordon and Dale Jarrett.

Sterling Marlin, Rick Mast, Dale Jarrett, Hut Stricklin and Michael Waltrip relax on the pit wall.

Bill Elliott had his day and his car shortened at Martinsville.

Every NASCAR Winston Cup team comes to the track ready to race,
but no team can prepare for weather like this.

A flat tire makes for an impressive light show during a night race.

Kenny Wallace and Terry Labonte look forward to the 1994 NASCAR Winston Cup season.

Jimmy Spencer and his Meineke Ford had some great runs in 1993.

This crew member sits perched on a tire awaiting the arrival of Michael Waltrip's Pennzoil Pontiac.

Bobby Labonte looks to equal the success of his older brother in 1994.

Winston
Cup Series
Goody's
Goody's
Winston Cup Series
Goodwrench
3
LUMINA
GOODYEAR
SIMPSON
3

Dale Earnhardt, Rusty Wallace and Ricky Rudd
mix it up at North Wilkesboro.

*Kyle Petty will look to become a force
in the upcoming
NASCAR Winston Cup season.*

*Six time NASCAR Winston Cup Champion
Dale Earnhardt will make a run at
King Richard's record in 1994.*

Mark Martin had an outstanding season in 1993. A championship in 1994 may be in the cards.

AUTOGRAPHS